Ron Prest

A NIGERIAN VILLAGER
IN TWO WORLDS

A Nigerian Villager in Two Worlds

DILIM OKAFOR-OMALI

FABER AND FABER
24 Russell Square
London

*First published in mcmlxv
by Faber and Faber Limited
24 Russell Square London W.C.1
Printed in Great Britain by
Latimer Trend & Co Ltd Plymouth*

DEDICATED
TO
THE YOUTH OF NIGERIA

Acknowledgement

I wish to express my sincere thanks to my great friend, Dr. P. E. H. Hair, formerly of the universities of Ibadan and Sierra Leone, now of the university of Khartoum, for the encouragement and advice he has given me, since 1953, in the preparation of this book.

Contents

INTRODUCTION   *page* 13

1. THE VILLAGE DIARY   19
2. VILLAGE GROWTH AND ORGANIZATION   32
3. BIRTH AND CHILDHOOD CEREMONIES   42
4. CARE OF CHILDREN   50
5. EDUCATION   58
6. THE COMING OF THE WHITE MAN   69
7. CHRISTIAN SUPPORTERS AND CHRISTIAN CON-
   VERTS   77
8. THE COLLAPSE OF LOCAL INSTITUTIONS   89
9. THE COMING OF THE CHURCH   93
10. DENOMINATIONAL STRIFE   101
11. THE BEGINNING OF MASS EMIGRATION   108
12. MARRIAGE   116
13. THE CHRISTIAN CHILD   128
14. OVERTHROW OF THE WARRANT CHIEFS   134
15. THE TOWN UNION AT WORK   147
16. CULTURAL PRIDE   153

Introduction

The author of this book has addressed it to his fellow-Nigerians. Written in the form of a life of the author's father, the book appeals to the younger generations of Nigerians, as they build up their great new country (the most populous in Africa, by a wide margin), to remember the past, and in particular the cultural achievements of their ancestors. The sincere patriotic feelings of the author, as well as his deep respect and affection for his father, will be obvious to all who open the book, and have helped to create a work to which it will be difficult for readers, Nigerian or non-Nigerian, to deny a sympathetic response.

Naturally, not every reader will wholly accept the author's interpretation of past events, or approve of all the ways in which Mr. Okafor-Omali believes that a culturally rich Nigeria can be maintained. On such complex topics there are normally many opinions—and it is usually profitable to have all these opinions openly expressed and publicly discussed. This book provides an opportunity for the discussion of the cultural future of Nigeria, starting from the author's analysis of the problem.

Though the book is addressed to Nigerian readers, one of its incidental merits is that many of the larger events described also took place (during the same period, the last century of history) not only throughout Nigeria but through-

Introduction

out the greater part of Middle Africa—from Dakar to Mombasa, from Lake Chad to the Zambesi. Non-Nigerian Africans will recognize such episodes as the following—the arrival of the white man's colonial army; the collapse of indigenous political units; the penetration and propaganda of Christian missions; the decay of traditional forms of life; the advent of economic opportunities for those daring (or unscrupulous) enough to seize them; the migration of young men to the towns; the formation of non-traditional (or pseudo-traditional) societies to link the dazed migrant with more settled and secure elements in society, the older generations of migrants and the homeland. Because of these common historical themes, I anticipate that the book will be widely read throughout Africa.

It is not possible in this place to say more about Ibo society—the society from whose revolutionary changes both Nweke Okafor, the hero of the book and his son, the author, emerged (together with a host of distinguished Nigerians, such as the President of the Republic and the Principal of the senior university)—than that it has been fortunate in having its progress delineated by two deeply honest works, one of historical interpretation, this book, and the other of fictional interpretation, the brilliant novel *Things fall apart* by Chinua Achebe (1958). The two works differ greatly in style, and slightly in period and theme (one describes an older man broken by the changes, the other a younger man accepting and benefiting from them). But in general they corroborate each other, and jointly provide one of the richest pictures of an African tribal society under the impact of intrusive global developments yet to be presented. What they lack in detail—and some of their detail must be supplemented, or even corrected, by reference to the standard works by European anthropologists—they more than make up for

Introduction

by the immediacy of their approach. These Nigerian writers have themselves experienced many of the changes they describe, though in neither case is their personal experience the literal basis of their story.

Mr. Okafor-Omali was born in 1927 at Port Harcourt, a town created out of a swamp a decade earlier by the British, to provide an outlet for the developing commerce of East Nigeria. The town population was completely immigrant: it was drawn from several neighbouring tribes and was therefore polyglot. I understand that, in the first flush of their enthusiasm for global progress, the author's parents barred themselves from speaking their mother tongue, Ibo, before their eldest son in his early years, who was instead spoken to in English or pidgin. In the author's later childhood, the family moved to Enugu, now the capital of Eastern Nigeria and a city with a population approaching 150,000—but again a new creation, a town founded on wasteland in 1914, an immigrant settlement drawing in this case its people mainly from diverse Ibo groups, which until the rise of nationalism were separate and often hostile. Against this background of urban revolution, the author was brought up and educated. During these years, his interest in the growing pains of Ibo society was aroused, as I discovered when I met him in 1952 and discussed with him what was then my own interest, the evolution of the urban society of Enugu. But during these years, and indeed up to the present day, the author has never had the fortune to live for any length of time in the 'home' village about which he writes so lovingly and longingly. As in other parts of the world, the evocation and evaluation of traditional rural society has come, very understandably, from those who feel themselves dispossessed, the early generations of townspeople. The most revealing and poignant episode of the present book is surely the occasion when the author, as a child, visits the 'home' village, and through ignorance and lack of a common language spurns and insults his grandmother. The shame the author experiences when he relives this episode has provided much of the emotional pressure which drove him to write.

The first draft of this book was written in Lagos, where the author lived after leaving Enugu. It was written while Mr. Okafor-Omali earned his living as a clerk, spent most of his spare time as a voluntary official of his 'tribal union' (the body his father helped to found), and lived in a single small room he shared with several work-mates. The writing of the book under these circumstances was an achievement of character, and in 1952–4 the subject, the cultural future of Nigeria, was largely original, as most Nigerian writers and the greater part of the reading public were, naturally enough, more concerned at that date with the political future of the country. Later versions of the book, which have, however, retained the main features of the first draft, were written in London, where Mr. Okafor-Omali has been attending a technical college in recent years and where his book has found, as he hoped when he planned his course, a publisher.

Mr. Okafor-Omali has written about the tug-of-war inside the contemporary African mind between innovation and tradition. It is commonly said that the Ibo people are the most innovatory in Nigeria, perhaps in all Africa; certainly their enthusiastic quest for modern education has put sons and daughters of Iboland in leading posts throughout the new Nigeria. The other side of the coin is the relative lack of interest, among the Ibo, in tradition. While this has sometimes been exaggerated it is undeniable that, as compared with the two other great peoples of Nigeria, the Yoruba and the Hausa, the Ibo have neglected their language and their traditional culture. It is a happy omen, therefore, that a discussion of the value of tradition in an innovating Africa should have come from a son of Iboland, who has himself, repeating the experience of his father and interpreting it more broadly, after massive exposure to innovation rediscovered another, more steadying, perspective.

In 1954 I had the privilege of visiting Mr. Okafor-Omali's home village, of meeting the elders, and of talking to the aged Ezeunọ. The old man told me, with emphatic gestures, that in his youth he had travelled no farther than a neighbouring village. 'In those days', he added, 'the world was different.' A changing world has led to villages everywhere being opened up, physically linked by widening roads, spun into the web of a global economy and modern society. A non-African may usefully conclude by reminding other non-Africans, and perhaps some Africans, that the basic problems of a changing Africa are not simply African and recent but are global and part of modern life. Mr. Okafor-Omali's message to Nigeria and to Africa is in accord with the wisdom of other continents. An Indian nationalist, Bankimcandra, wrote a century ago: 'There is no Hindu history. Who will praise our noble qualities if we do not praise them ourselves? When has the glory of any country been proclaimed by foreigners?' And it was the Anglo-Irish writer, Edmund Burke, who, in the course of a great essay on tradition, said that

'People will not look forward to posterity who never look backward to their ancestors.'

P. E. H. Hair

Sometime Research Fellow, West African Institute of Economic and Social Research, University College, Ibadan. Senior Lecturer in African History, University of Khartoum.

NOTE: o̤ differs from o and has the sound of 'aw'.

1. The Village Diary

CHRISTOPHER NWEKE OKAFOR, my father, was born in Enuagu village, part of a village-group called Enugwu-ukwu, which is to be found in the northern part of the country of the Ibo-speaking people, and in the administrative division of Onitsha Province, Eastern Nigeria.

He was intimately connected with social changes in his village-group from the 'Old World' of indigenous culture to the 'New World' of Western or European culture. In this process, four distinct stages appear: the first when the way of conducting village affairs was entirely indigenous; the next, when the white man came and a conflict broke out between the Indigenous Culture and Western Culture; the next again when Indigenous Culture gave way and the aping of Western Culture followed. The villagers at first accepted this third stage, but later the tragic implications of it dawned upon them. Then came the fourth and last stage, when individuals and later the whole people made strenuous efforts to revive and conserve the best of the indigenous customs and behaviour.

Christopher Nweke Okafor was born in the 'Old World' but became a pioneer of the 'New World'. Later he led his people as this account tells—'Back to the land'.

My father was a Postmaster. In 1928 he was transferred

from Port Harcourt, the principal port of Eastern Nigeria, to
a town called Bansara. There he worked for five years. The
house in which he lived was a well-built mud-walled bun-
galow, with six rooms, and roofed with corrugated-iron
sheets. Opposite the house and about fifty yards away was
the Post Office. At the back of the house were smaller houses
for Government workers. The market was about four hundred yards from our house.

Shortly after our arrival in this town, my mother secured
a market stall, where she sold merchandise in her capacity as
Company Agent. At this time I was a close companion of my
mother. About an hour after my father had gone to work in
the morning she would take me to the market. At lunch time
we came home together to prepare lunch for my father. Then
we went back to the market. It was always twilight when we
finally returned home.

My first vivid recollection of my childhood concerns events
which happened about the end of 1932. My mother one day
sent me to collect a parcel from my father. That was the first
time I was at the Post Office. My father was sending a message on the telegraphic circuit. I stood by him. He did not
know I was there. I was immensely fascinated by his ex-
quisite manipulation on the circuit. When he finished he
turned and saw me. 'What are you doing here?' was his
question. 'Mamma sent me to collect a parcel from you," I
replied. He gave me the parcel and I returned immediately to
my mother. The Post Office atmosphere made a remarkable
impression on me. I could not resist the urge to go and see
my father at work. If I told my mother she would not allow
me, so I slipped away without her knowledge. Soon I was
there. I could not go in, and was terribly disappointed that
I could not see much of the inside as the windows were high.
I was, however, content to linger around the door, watching

the coming and going of customers, and I carefully avoided
a position where my father could see me. But when I least
expected it, a stern voice said, 'What are you doing there?
Why are you not in the market with your mother? Where is
the parcel?' I remember I answered just one of these questions. 'Mamma has the parcel.' 'And what are you doing
there?' my father continued. I said nothing. 'Now go back
to your mother,' he ordered. Just then my mother appeared.
Her looks were grave and her eyes angry. 'What is wrong, my
dear?' inquired my father. 'I have come to tell you that I have
not seen Sigis for the past two hours. He has just dis-
appeared. I have made a frantic search for him all over the
market.' My father interposed, 'I have just seen him and have
already ordered him to join you. I wonder why he has come
here.' My mother stepped forward quickly and furiously
pulled me away by the hand. In the market I was greeted
with a fitting smack.

The next morning was a dramatic moment for the family.
My father was going to work. I stepped before him and
pleaded, 'Papa, Papa, I will go with you today, I will not go
with Mamma.' He looked straight into my face but had not
said a word when my mother urged him, 'Don't take notice
of Sigis, please. Go to your work.' She stepped forward and
pulled me away. I started crying and my father went to his
job. I wouldn't go with my mother to the market and continued crying. She was in a hurry and had to leave me behind.
My father heard me crying. He could not bear that for long,
and sent one of his workers to fetch me into the office. Once
I got there it was smiles and peace of mind for me again.
Shortly after, my mother came home to see how I was. My
father advised her to leave me with him.

The next morning I repeated my pleading and went to
work with my father. And so started my regular daily visits

to the Post Office. In the office there was excitement from time to time. I was friendly with the workers. I was happier with my Post Office friends than with my market friends. In the market they were mostly women, and I thought they were loosely dressed, very noisy and not as orderly as my mother. But my Post Office friends were smartly dressed men, and most of them spoke pidgin English. At first I was very shy and would talk to people only when they first talked to me. These conversations in pidgin English thrilled me greatly. Later I became 'the young talkative' at the Post Office. Any of the customers I encountered got a cheerful 'Hello!' from me.

Since my birth, my parents had lived in government quarters, a sort of multi-racial community. There the lingua franca was English and I learnt to speak English. Grammar or syntax was unknown to me but I remember I 'pidgined' the English language very well.

The two aspects of Post Office work that fascinated me most were the operation of the telegraphic circuit and the telephone. I always looked on with tense amazement when my father sent telegraphic messages and spoke on the telephone. I could not resist the urge to fiddle with these instruments. One day when my father was busy on the counter in the adjoining room, I thought I could do something to satisfy my curiosity. The telegraphic circuit desk was higher than myself, but I managed to get my hand over the circuit and tapped some of those sounds I was used to hearing. I heard my father shout, 'Who is doing that?' All eyes turned on me. 'Come and see for yourself,' said one of the workers. Soon my father appeared. 'What!' he sharply exclaimed. I caught his eyes and knew he disapproved of my action. 'Why have you done that?' he asked. 'I see you do it always,' was my reply. All the people around me burst into laughter. My father joined in too. I couldn't understand what the laughing was all about. Finally the warning came that I should never touch that instrument.

My next concern was the telephone. For two people to exchange conversation in that manner was a mystery to me. I was determined to speak on the telephone as I had seen my father do. Any time he used the telephone, I would watch him. He first made connections on the switchboard, then operated a dial before he took up the receiver to speak.

The European principal mercantile agent in the district was a personal friend of my father. He was very fond of me and always sent me presents of sweets and biscuits. Whenever he was out for a walk and passed by our house, I would run to him and enjoy a few minutes' chat. Sometimes I would tell him things I wanted, and he would send them to me. Of all the things he sent me, my favourite was a type of biscuit we called 'Star Biscuit'. This European's name was Mr. Jones, but I called him 'white man'. He was tall and wide with a picturesque moustache. My friend sent a Christmas present to me on the 24th December. To my great disappointment, the parcel contained no 'Star Biscuit'. I thought I must have my 'Star' for Christmas and I believed that if only I could get in touch with my friend, my hopes would be realized. The only medium for this was to use the telephone. I had seen my father telephone my friend many times, and I had taken note of the sequence of operations. I thought I would try that medium.

On Christmas morning, the office was opened for two hours. That was my only chance, I thought, but I was afraid my father would stay in the office all the time. However, when I looked, to my surprise and delight my father was back in the house, talking to my mother about the affairs of the day. I thought it was my chance. I dashed into the office through the back door, jumped on a chair, plugged in the switches, and operated the dial. I picked up the receiver and heard a voice. The line was through. I hastened to speak. 'Hello, Hello, my friend! Postmaster speaking! Send me "Star", please!' My friend spoke, but I did not understand. I was overcome by excitement, dropped the receiver, and ran from the office. The next minute I was in the house, where my father was still talking to my mother. Two hours later my friend sent my 'Star' through his messenger. I was delighted. Throughout Christmas, I was in very gay and buoyant spirits. It was one of the few childhood days in which I did everything I wanted and got everything I wanted.

The next day was Boxing Day. I had planned how to spend the day but little did I know that my freedom was coming to an end, and that I would pass the day in profound sobriety. My father went to work in the morning. My mother was busy in the kitchen preparing our lunch. Our housemaid was ironing the dress I would wear after lunch, and I stood by her admiring it. Suddenly my hand was furiously taken from behind. It was my father. Within seconds we were in the sitting-room. His were angry looks. Still holding my hand, he asked, 'Did you talk to the 'white man' on the telephone yesterday?' 'Yes,' I replied. He paused, gasping for a moment. 'When did you do that?' 'When you came back home,' I said. He continued, 'How did you do it?' I demonstrated how I did it. There was another but longer pause. 'Now tell me,' he said, 'who taught you to do that?' 'Nobody,' I said, still feeling unperturbed. Then came the last question —'How did you learn to do that?' 'I saw you do it,' was my reply.

My mother, unaware of what was going on, walked in. 'What is the matter?' she inquired. 'Come, my dear, I have a problem here,' said my father, his eyes still fixed on me.

The Village Diary

'What is it?' asked my mother. 'Mr. Jones telephoned me to inquire about Sigis and how he spent his Christmas yesterday. He said that Sigis telephoned him yesterday in the morning and asked for "Star Biscuits", so he sent his messenger with some biscuits.' 'What . . .! you telephone!' exclaimed my mother, terribly upset. She snatched my hand from my father's and continued, 'How did you do it, tell me! Tell me!' I said nothing. Turning to my father, she said, 'Hasn't he spoilt your work by that? How does Mr. Jones feel about it?' 'O no, not in the least. Mr. Jones understands. He was surprised that I was unaware of his telephoning and thought Sigis a clever boy.' 'Clever boy?' returned my mother. 'Yes, nothing has gone wrong this time. My concern now is to stop this sort of embarrassment. If he had misused the instrument and damaged it, that would make trouble. I didn't tell you what he did the other day. You know how high the telegraphic bench is; he got his hand over it and operated the circuit. He didn't know what he did but the sound he made was comprehensible. Both workers and customers were astonished when he said he did it just as he saw me always doing it.' 'Isn't that wonderful! But we must stop him interfering with your work. May I ask you now to leave him entirely to me,' my mother demanded. Then my father concluded, 'I will also discourage him from coming to my office. He is beginning to make a habit of it. I will have my eyes on him to find out what he is up to.' Turning to me again he gave his injunction, 'Look, Sigis, you must never come into my office again.' To discourage me the more he added, 'The White Man does not want you there.'

This sounded like a thunderbolt in my ears. I became sad and felt I had lost everything in the world. Quietly I walked out to the front of our house and remained there standing by the walls. My father had gone back to his job and my mother to the kitchen. While I was outside, amusing myself with pebbles, I looked up the road and saw my friend the White Man walking down the road. I had never seen him out at that hour of the day. My heart leaped with joy and I raced towards him. Just then my mother came out to fetch me in. When she saw me running, she thought I was trying to avoid her, so she ran after me, shouting appeals that I should come back. I continued running and misfortune came my way. I stepped into a ditch and fell down, bruising my face and arms. Up again quickly, I ran on. The White Man saw me fall and hurried to help. My mother was also running towards me. I soon reached the White Man and shouted at him, 'You no want me for office!' He quickly took my hand and examined my hurts. Then my mother arrived. The White Man inquired, 'What is the matter, Mrs. Okafor?' My mother told the story. 'Well, let's first look after his injuries and then I shall have a word with his father.' He allowed my mother to take me home while he went to the Post Office to see my father. Later both of them came to see me when my hurts were being dressed.

My injuries were serious and I became sick. It was six days to New Year's Day. The emphasis had shifted from child discipline to child health. I was in bed for three days. But on New Year's Eve I was well enough to join in the fireworks display.

It was early rising from bed on New Year's morning. The house cleaning done, and breakfast over, I dressed and was ready to leave for the New Year Service. Then a friend of my father came to wish us a happy New Year. He rode on a motor-cycle and was also going to the church. I insisted on going with him instead of walking with my parents. He put me behind him and off we went. We had not travelled one hundred yards when I slipped my right foot into the rear wheel spokes. I felt a dreadful pain and screamed. The cyclist stopped. I saw blood all over the ground. I heard the incredibly shocked voice of my mother saying, 'What can I do now!'

My next recollection was when I lay in bed. I moved my right leg and get another shocking pain. I cried. I saw white bandage all over my right leg. My mother came in within seconds, sat by me and tenderly comforted me. She talked to me about those things which aroused my interest. She told me that when I was well I could talk to my friend on the telephone. I beamed with a smile. She continued, 'You must get well soon, dear. You know it is only six days to your birthday. 'What is that?' I inquired. 'I mean the day you were born. Don't you remember last year when we killed a turkey and cooked rice? We all ate together. Don't you remember your friend brought you a big cake and you lighted candles around it? Don't you remember you had plenty of Star biscuits? Don't you remember?' she asked, holding me tenderly and stroking my hair. 'O yes, mamma, I gave James some biscuits. I gave Nwoye also. Oji begged me and I gave him. The light was beautiful.' 'That is right, dear, you do remember!' 'Where is the light now; and the cake; and the biscuits? Have you killed the turkey? I will eat the head,' I said. My mother continued, 'It is not now. I told you it will take place in six days' time, and then you can have everything you want.' I started again, 'Why is it six days' time? Can't we have it tomorrow?' 'Oh no, we can't have it tomorrow because tomorrow is not your birthday. Your birthday is 7th January and that is the only day we can do it.' 'What do you call it?' I asked. 'We call it birthday.' I repeated 'Birthday— and you said it is the day I was born?' I added. I was much absorbed in this new idea, but my mother suddenly changed the subject. 'You stay quiet. I wish to go to the kitchen. I shan't be long.' I quickly showed my disapproval. She looked around, went to the wall and brought a glass frame. She showed it to me but I did not recognize anything in it. She started to explain. 'My dear, look, this is your baptismal certificate.' She said other things about it which I do not remember. It was a very attractive certificate and I much admired it. "Isn't it nice?' she asked. I replied, 'Yes.' She continued, 'Now you can have a good look at it until I am back. It is yours, so keep it.'

My next visitor was my friend the White Man. That was his first visit to our house. I was delighted to see him by my bedside. My first reaction was to show him my baptismal certificate. 'Look, look!' I said very cheerfully. He looked at it and said, 'That is your baptismal certificate. Do you like it?' 'Yes,' was my reply. 'I also have one like that,' he added. 'Where ee dey?' I asked. 'It is in my home in England.' 'You eat biscuit and kill turkey too?' 'O yes, I do,' he replied. 'Na tomorrow you go do that?' I asked. 'Not tomorrow. My birthday is next month.' 'When be that?' I asked. 'Not long time,' he replied. 'You go give me cake and turkey?' 'Yes, I will send you some cake and nice things,' he promised. I was very pleased, and proudly cheering up, said, 'Only you and me get birthday.' 'No, everybody get birthday, your father get, your mother get, everybody get. Your birthday is the day mamma born you,' he commented. That was really good news to me. I reasoned that if I could get a promise of nice things on the White Man's birthday, my parents could promise the same, and I could look forward to something nice all the time. My father soon joined us to receive a question which he later told me much embarrassed him. 'Papa, Papa,' I said, 'what be your birthday? White Man tell me he get birthday.' I remember he quickly talked about subjects that he knew fascinated me, but avoided my question. Soon they left me. They were still within hearing distance when I shouted, 'Pappa, come what be your birthday?' They turned, waved their hands and went away.

I haunted my father with this question for many years. For a long time, he succeeded in avoiding an answer, but he knew that was not enough. When he thought I could understand, he gave me a full answer.

'I am not as lucky as you are to know my birthday and have a certificate to that effect,' he said. 'What do you mean?' I retorted. 'You know,' he said, 'I was born in the village. There was no reading or writing at that time, and so there was no record of the date I was born.' I was sad about this and looked at him pityingly. I just didn't know what to say. There was a pause, then he continued, 'But there is something I can tell you.' 'What is it, Papa?' I quickly cut in. 'I have some *idea* of when I was born.' I greeted this with a broad smile. He went on—'It is a difficult explanation but I will make it simple for you. I know the year and month of my birth but I am not sure of the day. Now this is what happened. When, in 1915, I asked my uncle the year of my birth, the old man took me to his yam-barn in which, he said, he had set yams seventeen times since he built it. And he said that he built it about four native weeks (four days make a native week) after the Qnwasatọ (Yam harvest) festival, and that I was born about eight native weeks before the festival. He was certain about this, because my Asa-nwa (naming) ceremony took place about four day before this festival.'

The Qnwasatọ festival still takes place about the month of August and formally marks the beginning of the harvesting period. It is celebrated with great feasting, when new crops, particularly of yam, are eaten. The highlight of the ceremony is the thanksgiving ritual procedure. Every family is expected to kill at least a fowl. The senior member of the family kills the fowl in his Obu (the father's sitting-house), sprinkles its blood on the Okpensi (the symbol of the family), and lifts his voice in thanksgiving to the ancestors of the family. He prays that they should continue to protect the family and give them the ability to live, to accumulate more wealth, and to build a greater community. Next, the feathers of the fowl are removed, not inside but outside the compound, and sprinkled on the threshold. This is done to demonstrate the determination of the people to forsake all evil in the coming season. Of the fowls killed for the occasion, at least one is roasted and reserved, while others are consumed at the day's feasting. The second day, the roasted fowls are produced by every family, and all the members of the extended family meet in the Obu of the senior elder to share them. As custom provides, particular parts of the fowl go to elders and women. This procedure is called Inya Okuku (handing round of fowl).

My father continued, 'My uncle told me that the year of my birth was a very remarkable one for him. In that year he made his greatest harvest of yams. As his barn could not contain his stock of yams, he decided to extend it. Because of his good fortune in that season, he contributed generously to my childhood ceremonies, such as Ito-nwa (presentation to family ancestors) and Asa-nwa (naming and presentation to the people). This evidence allows me to calculate as follows.' He interrupted, 'Go for your pencil and let's work it out together.' I arrived with my pencil and paper, and he continued, 'Seventeen harvests before 1915 must mean 1898. 32 days before August means June or July.' He allowed me to think over it and asked, 'Do you agree?' I agreed.

He continued, 'I was named Nweke after the market day of my birth. There are four days in the Ibo week; Eke, Oye, Afo and Nkwo. I was born on Eke market day and was named

The Village Diary

after it.' (Nwa (son) + Eke (market day) is shortened to Nweke.)

'It is therefore proper to state that I was born on an Eke day, in either the month of June or July, in the year of our Lord 1898. Do you now understand?' he asked, tapping his pencil on the table. 'Yes, I do. Thank you very much indeed.' Then I said, 'Wasn't your uncle wonderful to remember all this!' 'O yes, he had a fine memory, as had most of our elders in the village. Pen and paper they knew not, and so they kept records of events in their memory. This eventually constituted the village diary.'

This was how I first learned about the ways of the Old World in the village, by discovering my father's birthday. Now I shall describe other features in the traditional life of my people, by telling how my father grew up in the 'Old World'.

2. Village Growth and Organization

VILLAGE ADMINISTRATION

The primary unit of indigenous administration of Enugwu-Ukwu, the village-group into which my father was born, before the arrival of the white man, was the Extended Family (a man and his wife and small children, his grown-up sons and their families, sometimes his younger brothers and their families, sometimes even cousins and their families; all living in a single compound or in adjoining compounds). The next largest unit was the Quarter (a group of extended families claiming a common ancestor a few generations back). This unit is known among the Ibo as Umunna. Larger again was the Village, a group of quarters claiming a more distant common ancestor. Larger still was the Village-Group (often called 'town') claiming a yet more distant ancestor. There was effective organization at all four levels.

The administration of the various units was in the hands, in each case, of a council presided over by the senior man of the unit. The composition was such that every male member of the unit was represented. The council of each unit tried cases between members of the unit and took decisions within traditional limits. The council enforced regulations binding on the individual members of the unit. Units were often held collectively responsible for the misdeeds of their members.

Village Growth and Organization

When matters of village concern, such as the clearing of roads, land disputes and disagreements between sections of the village, were raised, all units were represented in the discussions. The representatives were traditionally the senior men of the units.

The senior man in a unit was not necessarily the oldest man. He might be the senior man in the senior line, and some of the men in the junior lines might be older than he. If the senior man was too much broken down by old age to exercise authority, he could delegate a relative to act for him. In councils, men of wealth and power as well as those with outstanding intelligence, even though younger, exercised influence. Though representation was traditionally by seniority, these exceptions made the councils rather less conservative in tradition than might otherwise have been the case.

OUR ANCESTORS

The first inhabitant and ancestor of Enugwu-Ukwu was a man called Okpalakanu. It is believed that his father was called Nri (after whom a town near Enugwu-Ukwu was named) and that he was Nri's eldest son.

Okpalakanu left his father's compound to live on a hill about three miles distant and there became the ancestor of Enugwu-Ukwu (which means Big Hill). His descendants were the founders of the villages within Enugwu-Ukwu. Okpalakanu was said to be very warlike. By his military tactics he occupied the hill site and he was able to subdue his enemies on many occasions.

My father was very proud of his ancestors, and was fond of relating the account of a war called the Ada war, to demonstrate their military skill. His narrative and gesture never failed to appeal to his listeners.

Village Growth and Organization

'The name Ada refers to a set of dwarfish but stoutish belligerent people who came from Item, Ohofia and Abriba Districts.' That was how he usually introduced the account. He would relax and continue: 'These people were good warriors but largely mercenaries. They attacked in great numbers.

'It is said that long before the white man came, one malignant individual, by name Okoli Ijọma of Ndi Ikelionwu, once hired a good number of Ada warriors and travelled to some villages in Udi District. There they attacked and plundered the people.

'News reached Okoli Ijọma about the military valour of the people of our town, Enugwu-Ukwu, and he resolved to go and challenge them too, to establish the supremacy of his army. It was said that a friend of his, by name Jojo Nubani, advised him not to attempt to invade our people. Okoli Ijọma became infuriated by this. 'You too do not believe in my greatness!' he addressed his friend. 'That is why I must go there, to make you know I am Ijọma.' He hurriedly despatched a message to our people announcing the date of his invasion, and warned that they must either surrender on his arrival, or perish at the point of his sword.

'On the eve of the appointed day, the Adas entered the town from the direction of my village. In the night they hid themselves in the thick bushes near the village, waiting for the dawn, when they would attack the villagers and continue their conquest further. The leaders and warriors of my village, as well as those of the adjoining village Akiyi, had earlier set up a system of watch-points along the borders, and the Adas were well shadowed. Women and children were hidden in the Strong Houses (Unọ Nga) and various hiding-places in the village. Sufficient food and water were provided for them in case the battle was unduly prolonged. The men filled many big pots with a poisonous species of cassava, poured water into them, and kept them in the compound of one Nkwaku Obele in Akiyi village. This compound was on the approach of the Adas. Many pots of poisoned palm-wine were displayed here and in adjoining compounds.

'This species of cassava does not cause instantaneous death. If eaten it makes the body languid. The poison in the palm wine does not kill but similarly incapacitates.

'The signallers and fighters took up various strategic positions, ready to seize any opportunity for a successful defence. At dawn, the Adas tiptoed into the village. They saw nobody as they advanced. Strangely enough, they could not trace the footprints of the villagers. For shortly after the villagers had retired to their hiding-places, a flight of pigeons landed in the village, and walked over the foot-paths. Instead of footprints of men, the invaders saw footprints of pigeons. They were completely deceived and concluded the villagers had fled.

'These war-mongers entered Nkwaku Obele's compound. Already very hungry, they pounced on the cassava and ate it and drank the water and wine. There was a spectacular stampede for this "menu". A great number of those who partook were rendered useless for the operation.

'The principal village war-signaller well concealed on the top of a tall tree, whose job it was to make a general survey of the situation and direct the attack, gave the signal. The villagers rushed out from their hiding positions and desperately attacked their invaders. Poor Adas! They were horrified. Many of them were killed or captured and the rest fled. The only serious casualty on our side was the loss of the son of Mgbo Ufo of Akiyi village.'

My father proudly concluded, 'This was a unique military success in Ibo local history. So ended the bold attempt of Okoli Ijọma and his men to attack my people. The conquest earned my people the reputation of "Ike Melu Ada", meaning the Power that humiliated the Ada. This was said to be the only disastrous defeat of the Adas, and from this time nothing was heard of these belligerent warriors.

'My people believe that the action of the pigeons was largely contributory to their victory, and particularly to the negligible casualty figure. For this reason, from that time, the pigeon was regarded as sacred and the villagers were forbidden to kill or eat it.'

THE ADVENTURE OF EZUNEBETE

Okpalakanu's eldest son was Ezunebete. He is said to have been very much like his father in appearance and in character. He was tall, robust, handsome, very courageous and warlike.

This was the period of petty warfare, slavery and kidnapping, so that it was rare for people to move in small groups a distance of more than half a mile without being fully armed or ready to challenge any enemy who might confront them. Ezunebete was, however, exceptional. He was so very confident in his military valour that he several times travelled far beyond his quarters when hunting alone. This practice was regarded as extraordinary. In one of his hunting expeditions, he discovered a site about a mile east of where he lived which was rich in fruits and vegetables. He preferred this site to his former almost barren hilltop habitation and decided to settle there, with his wife, daughters and sons. He made himself quite at home and built a shrine where he lived. This site is at present known as Ngwu Ajana (which means 'a sacred tree on sacred land'). The site of Ngwu Ajana was later occupied by one of his brothers, whose descendants formed Ire village.

In another hunting expedition Ezunebete travelled farther eastwards into a thickly forested area and had successful hunting. In addition to the rich vegetable products of this area, he eventually discovered a stream from which he could easily draw drinking water. This time he hastened to convey his family and belongings to this area and lived there permanently. This site is Enu-Agu ('high forest') village, situated in the east part of Enugwu-Ukwu town.

Though Ezunebete left his hilltop and Ngwu Ajana abodes to reside at Enuagu, for a time he regularly revisited these two places at festival times to direct ritual affairs in the two shrines, the Ngwu shrine at Ngwu Ajana and the Ana Enugwu shrine (Ana = the goddess of the land) of his father Ọkpalakanu. This Ana Enugwu shrine is the cult symbol which still unites all the villages in the Enugwu-Ukwu village-group, and we are thus certain that it was founded by Ọkpalakanu, the ancestor of Enugwu-Ukwu. And as it was customary for the eldest son to take over from his father his ritual rights, and since Ezunebete directed ritual affairs immediately after the death of his father, he must have been the Spiritual Head of Enugwu-Ukwu and thus the eldest son of Ọkpalakanu. However, Ezunebete eventually found it impossible to continue the duties at the Ana Enugwu shrine, and entrusted them to his brother Osili. But he was always consulted when important ceremonies were to take place in the shrine, and his descendants are so consulted up to the present day.

In a later generation a peculiar and exceptional circumstance occurred when a senior son was disinherited by his father. This is how it happened.

The three sons of Ezunebete married and had children. The sons at first lived together in their father's settlement of Enuagu, but when their families increased, their father allocated separate settlements to them. Ike was the senior son and inherited his father's settlement, Enuagu, and after the death of his father, directed ritual performance there. His two brothers Atuọra and Ọkandu, were allowed to found separate settlements near Enuagu. The descendants of Ike are today known as Enuagu, the name of their village. The descendants of Atuọra are called Umuaturọa ('the children of Atuọra'). The descendants of Ọkandu are called Akiyi ('the people by the side of the stream').

Ike had only one male child, Ezeunọ, but he was the father of eight sons. The descendants of these eight sons were the ancestors of the eight quarters (Umunna) of Enuagu village. The eight quarters are called after the eight sons—Nkwaku, Ọmali, Ale, Cheche, Obezi, Nwatu, Akpọra and Dajana. The oldest son was Nkwaku, but it must now be told how he lost his seniority rights.

Of all these eight sons, Cheche gave most assistance to his father. When, in time, the father thought it wise to give his children separate quarters to live in with their families, he started off by allocating land to only six of them. He made no allocation to Nkwaku, the senior son, or to Cheche. Cheche waited for a considerable time to see whether his father would extend the allocation to him or not. He was disappointed because he thought his father had overlooked him and did not appreciate his good services. When, shortly afterwards, his father as usual begged him to pick firewood for him, he refused and in addition gave up his other services to him. He then revealed his grievance to his mother, who reported it to the father. The father was very sorry, as he had not really meant to be unfair to him. He therefore called Cheche and Nkwaku to him. He said that he did not mean to be partial but was acting according to the dictates of his conscience.

The father, Ezeunọ, was at this time the owner of two compounds. While his own father was alive, Ezeunọ had built another house to live in, but, on his father's death, had transferred to his father's house. He now decided to give these two compounds to Cheche and Nkwaku. Speaking to Nkwaku, the senior son, he requested him to choose one of the two compounds. After much consideration Nkwaku chose, not his grandfather's compound, but the compound built by his father, which he considered more beautiful. With great surprise, Ezeuno said, 'My son, you have chosen wrongly. Why? You have preferred this fancy place to your heritage.' Turning to Cheche he said, 'I see the gods know how well you have served me, and your good nature. I think this is your compensation. My father's compound is now yours and I hope the same gods who mercifully gave it to you will give you the good spirit to have complete control of its affairs. Here is my Ọfọ (a staff representing authority) for you and your descendants.' Then he struck the ground with the Ọfọ, which action was meant to convey his words to his ancestors resting underground. From that time he allowed Cheche to direct all ritual proceedings even though he himself was still alive.

Cheche was the father of five children, Anyanọm, Okolofido, Agbiọgwu, Ọmali Ukam and Egbogoli. Their descendants form the five extended families of Cheche quarter in Enuagu village.

It was in this generation that the three brother villages of Enuagu, Umuatuọra and Akiyi (collectively known as Akanatọ) became an exogamous unit. They thought very much about their blood relationship and decided they should not continue to intermarry within the three units.

One of Cheche's sons was Ọmali Ukam, and he in turn had one son only, Ọkafọ Ọmali. This man had outstanding ability, and an inspiring character and outlook, and was very popular among his people. He was the father of five sons, one of whom was my father, Nweke, who is the hero of this book.

Thus, my father's genealogy was as follows:

NWEKE

son of

OKAFQ QMALI

(founder of the extended family of that name)

son of

QMALI UKAM

son of

CHECHE

(founder of the quarter of that name)

son of

EZEUNQ

son of

IKE

son of

EZUNEBETE

(founder of the village of ENUAGU)

son of

QKPALAKANU

(founder of the village group of ENUGWU-UKWU)

Nweke's Family Tree

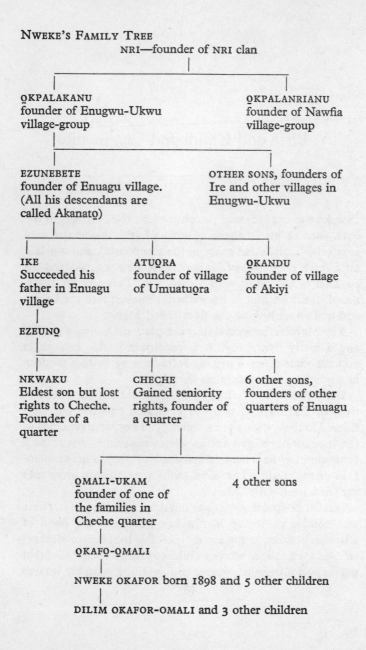

NRI—founder of NRI clan

OKPALAKANU
founder of Enugwu-Ukwu
village-group

OKPALANRIANU
founder of Nawfia
village-group

EZUNEBETE
founder of Enuagu village.
(All his descendants are
called Akanato)

OTHER SONS, founders of
Ire and other villages in
Enugwu-Ukwu

IKE
Succeeded his
father in Enuagu
village

ATUORA
founder of village
of Umuatuora

OKANDU
founder of village
of Akiyi

EZEUNO

NKWAKU
Eldest son but lost
rights to Cheche.
Founder of a
quarter

CHECHE
Gained seniority
rights, founder of
a quarter

6 other sons,
founders of other
quarters of Enuagu

OMALI-UKAM
founder of one of
the families in
Cheche quarter

4 other sons

OKAFO-OMALI

NWEKE OKAFOR born 1898 and 5 other children

DILIM OKAFOR-OMALI and 3 other children

3. Birth and Childhood Ceremonies

Nweke was born, as was the custom, in the open air, in the back yard of his mother's compound (this being the only comfortable concealed space in the compound), and was laid on a fresh plantain leaf. Immediately he acknowledged his position in the world with a shrill cry. This was the traditional signal for him to be washed, removed into the house, and laid on a plank on the floor called Mgbo.

The Mgbo is the special sleeping-place for both the mother and a newly born baby. It is constructed wide enough to accommodate them. They are forbidden by custom to sleep in any other place except on the Mgbo.

Had Nweke been born a twin, he would not have been so treated. The birth of twins or deformed children was considered in those days a great calamity. They were regarded as the incarnation of evil spirits whose mission it was to seek vengeance for the concealed evil deeds of the parents or members of the family. Therefore twins were thrown away into the 'Bad Bush' (Ajo Ofia).

It must be said that this was not done out of cruelty. There was nothing as strong in Nweke's people as the bond of affection between mother and child. But in this case mothers refused even to look at their children. It was their belief that nature had a definite course, and anything contrary was an abomination. It was believed that if such creatures were not destroyed, woes and calamities would be the lot of the people. To cast them away was a sign of repentance, and immediately afterwards a sacrifice was made to appease the vengeful spirit and to cleanse the compound. In those days it was an ill fate to have twins, but today it leads only to great feasting and merry-making. This is one of the results of the early work of the missionaries in this area.

CIRCUMCISION

Nweke was circumcised between two and three native weeks (eight to twelve days) after his birth, as custom dictates. There are no formal ceremonies attached to this practice. All children, male and female, are circumcised.

ITǪ-NWA CEREMONY (Presentation to family ancestors)

Till three native weeks (twelve days) after the birth of a child, custom did not permit the mother to eat with her husband. She could not appear in the husband's sitting house (Obu) and could not take part in any domestic work. Also she could not attend any funeral. She was expected only to feed the child and be at ease. Further, the newly born baby could not appear in the Obu. But when it was three native weeks old, the Itǫ-Nwa ceremony was performed. At this ceremony the Mgbo on which the mother and the child slept was washed and put away. Every compound was expected to have one or two of these to be used on any occasion of childbirth. Custom then permitted both the mother and child to sleep anywhere. The mother, now cleansed from her childbirth pollution, could attend to her husband and eat with him. She was free to take part in domestic work and other activities.

43

And most important, the child was formally brought into the Obu. This ceremony was principally the concern of the Umunna (quarter) of the child.

At the Itọ-Nwa ceremony, in the presence of all the members of his Umunna, Nweke was formally taken into the Obu by his mother. The senior man in the Umunna then officiated and received him. He poured a libation of palm wine and kola on the Okpensi (see page 47), said prayers, presented him to his ancestors and blessed him. The members of the Umunna were feasted with wine and boiled yam and vegetables.

The occasion on which Nweke was received was said to be very remarkable; there had never been one as grand in his father's compound. We have already seen the reason for this —his uncle had had an unusually successful harvest. He therefore did not hesitate to contribute plenty of yams and palm wine for Nweke's Umunna.

This period was a continued period of feasting in the compound. Four native weeks (sixteen days) after his Itọ-Nwa ceremony, i.e. seven native weeks (twenty-eight days) after his birth, the Asa-Nwa ceremony followed.

ASA-NWA CEREMONY (Naming and presentation to the people)

The Asa-Nwa ceremony is the naming ceremony and is far more elaborate than the Itọ-Nwa. It is the concern not only of the Umunna, but of the whole village. Friends and relatives are usually invited from other villages, and even from outside the village-group. The Umunna of the mother is also specially invited. Before this ceremony, though the mother is free to take part in domestic work, she is not permitted to attend the market.

Birth and Childhood Ceremonies

Parents and grandparents are principally concerned in the naming of the child. Each may give a name to the child. Any other person approved by the family is also at liberty to give a name, and will then present special naming gifts to the child. In some cases, four or five people give names. One might wonder how it is possible for a child to answer to so many names. But it often happens that one popular name displaces all the other. This is generally decided by the mother, who refers to the child by a favourite name. The child learns from its mother, and eventually the whole village accepts the name. People who give names and wish the child to be known and called by that name make a special request to the mother with presents. But mothers are so influenced only under special circumstances. In some cases, however, the child uses both a first and second name.

Seven native weeks after Nweke's birth, the Asa-Nwa ceremony was performed. There was a grand assemblage of people. The senior man of Nweke's Umunna presided. After the traditional breaking of kola nuts, Nweke was handed over to the senior man, who formally presented him to his people, and he was greeted with vociferous cheers. As the parents and others gave him names, the senior man announced them to the people. Next, still as custom provides, he put into his hands a hoe and a matchet, the chief farm implements, and said, 'My son, with these farm implements your father lived well. We call on you to acquaint yourself with them properly and be hard working. We wish you good fruits of your labour. Live, grow, and wax strong.' Drinks and food were served at the gathering.

The senior man of his family gave the name Nweke and his mother often called him by this name. Hence other children learnt it, and it soon became his popular name.

Birth and Childhood Ceremonies

HOW NAMES ARE GIVEN TO CHILDREN

The day of birth, special circumstances at the birth, or events occurring at the same time, generally suggest to parents names for their children. This can be illustrated by the names which Nweke himself, in later years, gave to his children. When his wife delivered her first child, the author, she laboured continuously for three complete days. Nweke was greatly worried about what might happen to his wife and the child at this difficult time of childbirth. Everybody, including the midwife, grew exceedingly anxious. But at 1 p.m. on the third day of her labour—the sun at its zenith full and bright—she smoothly gave birth to a male child. Nweke was in his working place but hurried home when the news reached him. The child was born strong and had a pleasing appearance. Hence, Nweke was always fond of him. At his baptism he gave him a second name Dilinyelum (Dilim for short) meaning: Be with me. His wife, recollecting her continued agony during her labour, believed that God had helped her. She therefore felt bound to express her feelings by giving him a third name, Chukwuemeka, meaning: God has done well.

In Nweke's village, children are generally described by their mothers' name because of the polygamous nature of the society. For example, if a mother's name is Nwije and the child's name is Okoye, he is generally referred to as Okoye Nwije.

Nweke's mother's name was Ugada, and by this system he was popularly known from childhood as Nweke Ugada. In any section of the village-group he was identified by this name. The popularity of his mother was in his early days responsible for his own popularity. Had he been referred to as Nweke Okafor no one would have recognized him.

Birth and Childhood Ceremonies

To complete his birth ceremonies, his mother made a formal presentation of herself at the market, and became free to attend the markets and go anywhere. This ceremony is called Afia Nwa.

AGU CEREMONY

The next childhood ceremony is that called Agu, or Igba Agu. There is no fixed time for it but it is performed at the convenience of the father or his representative. It is not necessarily accompanied by feasting. The father invites a diviner, who names the ancestor whose reincarnation the child is. When this is determined, a big dumb-bell-shaped piece of wood called Okpensi is prepared to represent this ancestor of the child. In the Obu, the Okpensi of all the members of the family are kept together. On them kola and libations of palm wine are poured, and to them prayers are said on behalf of any member of the family.

When the senior man in a family kills fowls, he gives the ancestors their share and asks them to make the meal nourishing by sprinkling the blood on the Okpensi and sticking patches of feather to it.

THE ỌFỌ INSIGNIA

After this ceremony, the Little ọfọ is provided for the child. The Little ọfọ is the ritual staff of each individual in the family. The staff is a branchlet of a sacred tree.

The ọfọ is a symbol of truth and guidance and represents the ancestors. It is given to the child to bring him nearer to his ancestor, who is his spiritual guardian. There is also the family ọfọ which protects the whole family and is held by the senior member of the family. The last type of ọfọ is that held by only titled men. It is the title staff of public authority. The titled men are the leaders of public opinion. It is believed that if they spoke falsely, as holders of ọfọ they would be killed by the ancestors. The efficacy of the ọfọ is so much esteemed that whoever denies any allegation is brought to swear on it, and if he swears falsely it is expected that evil will come on him.

The diviner looked into Nweke's case and announced that he was the reincarnation of his grandfather Ọmali Ukam. Nweke was then given his Little ọfọ.

AMANWULU CEREMONY

The next and final childhood ceremony is that called Amanwulu. Like the Agu, there is no fixed time for it. This ceremony permits one to take a title at a later date. It is the equivalent of a certificate or passport to travel. Thus Nweke completed his childhood ceremonies.

He had done the Itọ-Nwa, which qualified him to enter his father's house (Obu), and he had been formally presented to his ancestors.

He had done the Asa-Nwa, by which he took a name, and he had been formally presented to his people and wished a successful life.

He had done the Agu, by which the Diviner proved he was the reincarnation of his grandfather Ọmali Ukam, and he took his Little ọfọ.

He had done the Amanwulu, which qualified him to take a title when he was prepared.

These are the responsibilities of any father to his son. The father must also help the son when he wishes to marry. But other matters are the personal responsibility of the son, for instance, the taking of a title. However, Nweke, because he became a Christian, could not take a title.

Birth and Childhood Ceremonies

The custom of inheritance is that the father's property passes to his eldest son, and the mother's property to her youngest son.

The eldest son is called the Ọkpala and he represents the father, manages his property, controls his compound and holds the family ọfọ. He is expected to direct the property in the best interest of the other children. The most important part of the father's property is the land. This is communal property, and no member of the family has the right to alienate any part of it without the consent of all the other members of the family.

The mother's property may include her house and the adjoining garden (every wife has a house in her husband's compound), her personal farm land, palm trees, livestock and cooking utensils.

Nweke was the third and the youngest son of his mother and therefore inherited her property. He also had a share in the communal land of the village and eventually acquired personal land.

4. Care of Children

When he was thirteen days old, custom permitted Nweke to sleep anywhere and no longer on the first sleeping place, the Mgbo. His next sleeping place was more luxurious—a mat on the bedstead, a mud platform, in his mother's house.

He had no other nourishment than the breast and sips of water till he learnt to eat.

RESPECT FOR HIS MOTHER

According to his mother, when he was about three months old he was strong enough to take his position on her back. She told me that for a short period after this time he was always with her—feeding on her lap and sleeping on her back most of the day while she did domestic work. He expressed dissatisfaction whenever he was away from his mother. Nweke's people regarded this period of life as important, because during it was formed the bond of affection between mother and child. Mothers were always treated with honour and respect by their children. Their opinions were seldom disputed. Sometimes there might be misunderstandings, but they were soon forgotten. It was the height of indignity for anybody to hold an altercation with his mother. Anybody who neglected his mother was completely condemned in this society. Today, most people still regulate their behaviour in

50

accordance with their mothers' wishes. It is common to hear people in difficulties say, 'Oh! If it were not for my mother, I would have finished my life in the river and put an end to these worries.'

BABY-NURSE

Nweke was only four months old when his mother entrusted him completely to the care of a baby-nurse. Baby-nurses were generally children of about eight to ten years. It was their duty to take care of the child and keep him playing while the mother was busy in the compound or at the farm or market. Every time the child expressed his feelings of hunger by crying, the nurse poured sips of water into his mouth. This gave him some satisfaction and it was repeated till the mother was back home to give the breast.

This work was usually done by members of the child's family or extended family, or by a close relation of the mother with good personal qualifications. It was a matter of pride for children to have such an assignment and they were happy to be relieved, to some extent, from domestic work.

NWEKE TRAINED TO ASSOCIATE WITH OTHER CHILDREN

Nweke, like other children, had his mother as his best companion till he was about three years old. The period between births was usually three years, and then the first child was expected to give way to the next. When the next child came, the mother's attention went more to him, while the older child was expected to be in the company of his playmates. Some children after this period still tended to attach themselves to their mothers with their constant worries. Some mothers disliked such inconvenience, and in an-

noyance would say peremptorily, 'Will you go and join your
mates or do you think you are not yet above the age of
suckling? Will you get out!' In the event of the child's being
stubborn, he was forced out of the mother's house. In many
cases he would remain outside the gate of the mother's compound, crying and beating himself on the ground. A relative,
or sometimes the mother, would eventually come to pick him
up and stop him from crying. Most children with non-
indulgent mothers behaved in this way not more than three
times before they learnt to take their right place among their
fellow children. Nweke took his proper place among his fellow
children at the proper time. He then watched others and
developed more quickly than if he had been always with his
mother. Children at this period begin to think less of their
dependence on their mother, and it may be said that this
marks the beginning of the individualistic tendency in
Nweke's people.

NWEKE GUARDED IN THE 'STRONG HOUSE'

It was the daily routine for men and women to leave home
to work on the farm, or to go to the market. Until they were
old enough to work with them, children were always left
behind. It is interesting to note what happened to them at
home while the parents were away.

This was the period of petty warfare and kidnapping and
it was the practice for an invader to attack a compound and
kidnap the children in the absence of the parents. Sometimes
the invader was from a distant place, but often he was a
hostile neighbour. To conceal the children from such invaders, a special house called Unọ Nga was built at the centre
of the compound, and there the children were kept till the
parents returned.

Care of Children

The compound had a mud wall round it, with a narrow entrance gate, whose door was made of strong iroko wood. The gate faced the Obu, the father's sitting house, to enable the father, or any person sitting there, to see quickly anyone coming into the compound. To make sure that everyone entering the compound was announced, objects capable of making sharp noises when touched were hung on the door. Often iron gongs were used, and the slightest touch on the door was heard within.

A few years ago, I entered the compound of the oldest man in the village, a man renowned for his valour in his younger days, and I left open the gate of the compound. The old man looked hard at me and said, 'My boy, when I was like you, I did not make such a mistake. In our time, I do not think you would have passed through a gate without taking care to shut it. I do not blame you, this is the white man's age when there is no more danger.'

Within the compound, the wife's house was also walled round, so that should an invader get into the compound he could not easily penetrate to the Mkpuke, the wife's house where the children live with their mother.

Moreover, at the centre of the compound a 'Strong House' was built. This house was single-roomed, the area about 10 ft. by 10 ft., with thick walls. Only one narrow door led into it, and the few small openings for ventilation were made high up on the walls. The ground floor had a ceiling of mud at a height of about 12 ft. The walls were built up another 3 ft. and then roofed with mat. There was therefore both a ground floor and a first floor. The children were locked in the ground floor room when their parents went to the farm or to the market. This made it extremely difficult for invaders to molest the children.

This Uno Nga was also used for other purposes. Valuables

and war materials were kept in it. In wartime, the movement of enemies outside was watched through the small holes on the walls of the first floor. Entrance into the first floor was only by a ladder through a narrow opening in the ceiling of the ground floor. The ladder was removed immediately after use, and hidden in a corner of the room.

Prisoners of war were tied up near the Unọ Nga. They not only had their hands tied, but were fastened by the legs to a mud block called Ọgba near the house.

Not every compound had this building. It was expensive to construct, and one was sufficient for a group of compounds. There was none in Nweke's father's compound, but his children were concealed in one in a neighbouring compound.

NWEKE'S HEALTH IN CHILDHOOD

Nweke's mother told me that he was born strong and robust. She was very emphatic about this. When I asked her why she laid such stress on the words 'strong' and 'robust', she said that it was a source of great pride to mothers of that time to have healthy children. The ill health of children was a great embarrassment to mothers. She remembered how healthy Nweke had been and how happy she then was that he did not have the troubles which many other children had. Of course she realized how much easier it was for mothers today, when the ailments of children could be treated more effectively and easily. But although many modern cures for diseases had been introduced, she thought the physical sturdiness of the people had deteriorated.

This seems to be true. In past times, people prided themselves on their physique. They worked hard under the sun and defied the weather. These exercises and exposure to the sun made them stouter and stronger, and they were tougher than the people of this time, who spend less time under the sun and more time indoors and who therefore develop jelly-like features.

THE CARE OF SICK CHILDREN

The care of children in those days was the individual responsibility of the mother. The commonest ailment with children then was fever. As soon as the mother observed the symptom of high temperature, she carefully and skilfully pressed the stomach to feel whether there was constipation or not. If the child was constipated, she gave him a purge. It was the general belief that with a free stomach all ordinary ailments of the body would disappear.

The purge was the juice of a leaf called Kpupku Nmia. A child requires just a small quantity of this liquid. If the illness continued, a further concoction of leaves was administered. If the child was still sick, the mother became very worried and consulted her husband and women of experience, who could recommend some other form of treatment. If the condition became severe, as a last resort a doctor was consulted. He was a diviner who could find out if any evil deed had been committed for which the gods required appeasement. It was the belief that any severe illness was an expression of anger by the gods. The diviner always had something to say, and would after due consultation with his apparatus make his declaration.

NWEKE AND THE DIVINER

Once Nweke fell ill and the Diviner was consulted. He said that Nweke's grandfather, whose reincarnation he was, demanded a feast for the children in the compound in honour of Nweke. First, however, a white cock, two kola nuts and a keg of palm wine, he said, should be offered to the ancestor at a shrine in the village. In addition, he recommended that Nweke's body be smeared with camwood and a special concoction.

His mother got these things ready, and on the appointed day appeared before the priest of the village shrine. Some members of Nweke's family accompanied her to the shrine. The priest took up a kola and said the usual prayers. 'We have come to appease this boy's ancestor through you (the shrine). With this kola we pray you to harken unto our demand of this morning and let this boy enjoy his portion of life.' The priest then split the kola, placed a piece on the special stone on the mud shrine, and shared the remaining kola with the members of Nweke's family who were present. The other kola nut he kept for himself. He also poured libation of wine on the shrine. Finally he killed the cock and sprinkled the blood around the shrine. Patches of feathers were stuck to the drops of blood. The remaining palm wine was drunk by the priest and the members of the family. Nweke's mother cooked the cock in a pot and presented it to the children of the compound. Finally, the concoction recommended by the diviner was applied to Nweke's body the following day. Four days after the ceremony, Nweke recovered from his illness. According to native belief, the sacrifice appeased the gods, who allowed the full curing effect of the concoction. This method of treatment is now giving way to modern medical attention.

DEATH OF NWEKE'S FATHER

When Nweke was about three years old, his father fell ill and died. His mother continued to live in her husband's compound with her husband's other wife, and the children of the two wives grew up together. Nweke's mother worked hard on the farm to grow food for her children. She also made money by trading. Her dead husband's brothers helped her with the training of Nweke in his early days.

5. Education

The training of a child was the concern of the mother till he was about six years old. Before Nweke was a year old, he was taught to chew mashed cooked yam and gradually he learnt to eat without assistance. He was compelled to wash or clean his hands before he ate, and if any food fell on the ground, the dirt was carefully removed before it was eaten. He therefore soon learned to keep his food clean. At the same time he was taught obedience. His mother or other members of the family would give him a piece of yam or fruit, and then demand it back again. Nweke usually obeyed, but occasionally, when he felt the gift very dear to him, he was reluctant to give it up, and pressure had to be brought to bear on him to do what was against his will. He was also taught to refrain from talking while eating, and to say 'thank you' for any gift made to him. As soon as he learnt to speak fairly well, his mother sent him on minor domestic errands.

But when he joined his fellow children in sweeping his mother's house and compound, he did so of his own free will. This was the first business in the morning and Nweke, like many other children, then asked what next he could do for his mother. His mother's expression of delight when he did an errand quickly, and her scolding when he was slow at it, soon taught him to carry out all her instructions promptly.

Education

He grew up obedient and respectful, and as body and mind developed, he assisted his mother more and more in the strenuous domestic labour. With a small pot specially provided for him, he fetched water from the stream. At noon, he collected firewood in the company of other children.

Continuing his education, he learnt to light the fire for his mother and to roast or boil yams for himself. And the traditional stories, which were told to all children on moonlit nights, provided Nweke with moral education.

The shining moonlight was alluring to all—men, women, boys and girls. They enjoyed story-telling, wrestling and singing till late in the night. Nweke was still an infant, and as long as they were infants, boys and girls played together. They played under the watchful eye of the older children, those who were in the second age grade, and they were instructed by them what they should do and not do in their moonlight games.

Story-telling was always part of the moonlight play. The children sat in a ring with the story-teller at one end. As he told stories, the children listened attentively and joined in the choruses when the stories were sung. Many children had favourite stories and would request to hear them again and again. These stories moulded the minds of the children. Here are some instances of the type of story Nweke heard.

THE TWO SISTERS

'Once there lived a very wealthy man. Instead of marrying one wife, and then waiting some years before marrying another, as other men do, he married two wives from two different villages on the same day, and they came to his house together. In front of his kinsmen, he spoke to the two new wives and said that he had taken them together for a reason.

Education

He had seen and heard, he said, many quarrels in polygamous families, and these were mainly due to the domineering attitude of the first wife or else to the insubordination of the junior wife. To avoid this, he had arranged matters so that neither of his wives could claim superiority over the other. Hence they would regard each other as equals and he and they would live together happily. It happened as he said. They lived happily together and after about a year each wife was brought to bed of a female child. These children were exceedingly beautiful and looked astonishingly alike. Their father made a great feast and named them Anyanwu (sun) and Ọnwa (moon).

'When they grew up, they loved each other, and behaved well towards each other. Their father was pleased, since his theory appeared to work.

'But it happened that one of the wives gave birth, this time to a male child, while the other was not even pregnant. The mother of the one child grew worried since her companion had out-done her by having two children. Then she began to hate the other woman and at length to quarrel with her. She became even more angry when the woman she hated did not take the quarrels seriously, and she decided to do her serious harm, by killing the woman's daughter Anyanwu. She prepared a poison which she gave to this girl and the girl died suddenly. Everyone in the village was sad when they heard the news and Anyanwu's half-sister Ọnwa refused food and wept bitterly day and night. Then, one day, as she was walking through a small farm near the village, a voice came to her from above, which was like that of Anyanwu. The voice came again, this time more distinctly, and it sang sadly the following words:

' "Ọnwa! Ọnwa! Ọnwa!!! My beloved sister, your mother took away my life suddenly. She has done the worst she

60

could. Please take heart and comfort yourself. It was poison from the cruel hands of your mother that killed me." When Ọnwa heard this she grew frantic. Running back home, she spread the news and pointing to her mother said, "Kill me too!", and continued to weep bitterly. At night she stole out of her house and was found the next morning dead in the village stream.'

The purpose of this story is plain. There was always jealousy and quarrelling between half-brothers and sisters in a polygamous family, but this was controlled, unconsciously of course, by the impression made on the minds of children by such stories as that of the love between the two half-sisters Anyanwu and Ọnwa.

Nweke was particularly influenced by this story, as he came from a polygamous family. His father had two wives, and like Anyanwu and Ọnwa, whose friendship he admired, his thought was always how to keep peace with his half-brothers and how to prevent quarrels.

Another story continues with the relationship between brothers and sisters.

THE TWO BROTHERS

'Once upon a time there lived two sons of a king, Chike and Nwike. Chike was a quiet and good-looking boy with a very thoughtful disposition. Nwike was uncommonly handsome and well made, but he was full of talk and careless in behaviour.

'The king was equally fond of both sons. To encourage them to understand and love each other, he always assigned duties to them together and gave equal presents to them. One day he sent them to a stream to collect some herbs for him. Soon after their arrival, an old woman came down to the stream with a basket of breadfruits. The woman started washing the breadfruits, and turning to them said, "My good young princes, lovely things you are, and equally lovely is your father, whom I knew from his early years. If you are really good boys you will not hesitate to help an old woman at work." They had learned to be kind and helpful, so they completely took over the work from her. The work finished, she addressed them again—"Thank you, good boys. I know you are here on an errand, but your father will not be angry with you if you tell him you returned late because you carried my basket home for me, an old woman." They agreed to assist her.

'Her home was a good distance off, and, on arrival, they found that to enter her room they had to go through a series of winding passages. Then she offered them a seat and went away. Wise Chike watched the old woman carefully, since he began to feel that she did not mean them well. He therefore warned his brother that, if the woman brought food, they ought to compel her to eat with them, and not eat until she had eaten.

'Coming back, she brought food and in very soothing language presented it to them. Careless Nwike began to eat regardless of his brother's warning. One of his fingers was immediately paralysed. But Chike would only eat what the woman ate. Now this old woman was a fairy disguised, and wished to kill these boys. Chike sensed this and was anxious to leave. But since it was late, and they were afraid to go home in the dark, they slept in the woman's house.

'Before dawn the following day, Chike woke Nwike and told him it was time to run away, otherwise they would be killed. He recited some magic spells: "You doors, you gates, open and shut as we pass along." The doors, which were locked, opened and closed as they passed. The old woman immediately pursued them. Since they had run far away she had to use her magical power. She took out a horn and sounded a magical note which ordered Nwike, who was already caught by the poison she had put in the food, to die. "My horn, my horn, knock down Nwike for me. Knock him down, knock him down. I have already got him." She blew. Chike heard the sound and saw Nwike fall down dead. Chike ran away into the bush.

'The old woman found Nwike dead and was happy. She ran home to get a calabash to collect his blood, and left by his body her magic charms, including her horn. Chike seized the opportunity to save his brother. He ran out of the bush, took the horn and sounded a different tune. "Nwike, get up! Nwike, get up!! and run away with me." Nwike got up and they ran towards their home. They arrived home late in the evening, to be received with joy, for the whole town was anxious about the safety of the two princes. And Chike kept the old woman's magic horn.

'When it came to relating the story of their adventure, Nwike did all the talking and attributed the success of their adventure to himself. He was highly honoured for his supposed bravery. The following day, he was dressed in princely robes, and carried to the market-place, amidst dances and cheers, for a ceremonial parade. Nobody paid attention to Chike, who sat quietly by the fireside, thinking of the treachery and ingratitude of his brother.

'But as Nwike was showing off at the centre of the market, Chike took the horn and blew the tune the old woman had blown, and Nwike immediately fell down dead. Sorrow succeeded merriment in the market.

'When Nwike's funeral was being prepared a wise palm wine tapper approached the king and suggested that he ask the prince by the fireside, who had not said a word, for his own version of the story of their adventure, which perhaps had something to do with the sudden death of Nwike. At first Chike refused to make a statement. Then at last he took up the old woman's horn and blew his own tune, which restored Nwike to life. The true story of their adventure was then told, and Chike was rewarded with the highest title in the land and proclaimed the heir to the throne.'

The moral of this story was pointed out by the story-teller: 'When your brother has done you good, thank him, and think how you can help him too. Thus you will be useful to each other.' He added, 'Anyone like Nwike, who falsely tries to take the glory due to another, will surely be punished. Do not tell your mother that you swept her house when she went to the market, if it was not you who really did the work.'

Another story warns children to run errands quickly.

WHY MEN DIE

'God created the world with all its inhabitants and beauties.

'One day he thought of the fate of man. He called a tortoise and a dog, and sent them to the people in the world. To the dog he said, "Go and tell the people in the world that they will live and never die!" To the tortoise he said, "Go and tell the people in the world that they will live and die." God was thinking of these two alternatives for man, but could not decide which he would allow. He therefore decided that he would despatch these two messages to the world, and which-ever reached the people first would operate. He sent the dog and the tortoise with the messages, and he sent them away at the same time.

'To begin with, the dog ran faster than the tortoise, and would have brought good news to the world had he continued at the same rate. But when he had gone about half-way on his journey, he saw a pot of oil by the wayside. He was attracted by it, and, with the confidence that he ran faster than the tortoise, felt that he could enjoy part of it. He intended to watch to see the tortoise pass, and then overtake him again. But he found the oil so delicious that he did not notice the tortoise pass. When he was satisfied with the oil, he sauntered into the world, confident that he was to do a good work. But, to his great astonishment, the tortoise had already reached the destination and delivered his message.

'The people, however, did not like the tortoise's message and appealed to God. But he turned down their appeal with regret.'

The story concludes, 'If the dog had not loitered on the way, the fate of man today could have been to live and never die. So you can see that it is not good to loiter when you are sent on an errand, but to go straight away and do it.'

Children were also warned not to be lazy, but to work hard at their farming lessons.

An Idle Prince

'There once lived a king, who was very rich as a result of his labours. But his son, on the contrary, was very lazy, which made the king very unhappy. So he advised his son to attend his farm regularly and to join in the work. Thus he would learn to take charge of it, and keep up his wealth after his father's death. But the prince did not pay heed to his father's warnings, but was mainly concerned with putting on gorgeous princely apparel and gossiping everywhere under the escort of his father's slaves.

'At length the wealthy king died, and immediately a peasant living near the king's farm claimed the whole farm. The prince could not identify his father's land, and therefore could not make a strong protest to the peasant occupying his father's property. He exhausted the amount of money in his possession, and, when nothing more was forthcoming, he wept bitterly for his mistakes in the past. His kind father heard his voice and was moved with pity. He pleaded to God to send him back to the world to settle the matter rightly. But the peasant prayed to God that no dead man should rise again. The prayer of the peasant was heard, and so the king was not allowed to rise again.

'The idle prince lived unhappily, depending on his father's slaves for his daily bread—he who formerly walked about in gorgeous apparel under their escort.'

From such stories, various ideas and morals were inculcated into the minds of children.

SECONDARY EDUCATION

At about the age of seven, Nweke passed to his next tutor, his uncle, from whom he acquired more knowledge of farming, local history and language. His uncle took a special interest in him and was his best friend.

One bright morning, after the usual domestic work and breakfast, he was called upon to accompany his senior relatives to the farm. He leaped with joy and was ready to join the team in no time. On the way to the farm, he carried a senior relative's hoe. At the farm, he was employed either in removing grass or in running some minor errands. As his muscles developed, he learned the use of the matchet and the hoe in clearing the bush, he learned to make ridges, he learned to make mats for roofing. And he also learned to plant yams, to train the tendrils, to plant corn, to weed and to mark the farm boundary. Thus, within a short time he became a good worker on the farm.

Education

The farmers usually returned home in the afternoon. After resting a little, Nweke accompanied his uncle to various appointments, carrying his stool for him. The appointments included family meetings, feasts, ceremonial performances at the shrine, and sports such as wrestling contests and dances.

By accompanying his uncle, Nweke had the privilege of meeting senior men and of listening to many of their conversations, their stories, and their proverbs, some of which he learnt.

It was rare then for a child to mix with the elders and hear the traditional stories. A child like Nweke, who did, increased his knowledge of traditional history and village language.

VILLAGE PROVERBS

These old men had a peculiar fashion of making formal speeches in proverbs, so that only those conversant with the proverbs could follow their discussions.

An interesting incident happened in the olden days, which will illustrate how these proverbs were used and how they could be misunderstood.

The story goes thus.

Once, Nweke's people allied with a neighbouring town to invade and overthrow another neighbouring town. They agreed to do this on a certain day. Nweke's people told their allies to act according to the proverb—'Onye biako nya nwulu obu naka!'—which means, 'Everyone who is coming should come with the Obu!'

Obu is the name for the African cuckoo, which cries out just before dawn. By its cry people know that day is coming. Hence, by this proverb, Nweke's people meant that both parties should assemble in the morning, before dawn.

But the neighbouring town took the proverb literally. They

assembled at the correct time, but, instead of going to meet Nweke's people, went out into the bush, hunting for cuckoos!

At the appointed time Nweke's people, not seeing their colleagues, carried out the attack alone. It was not until after dawn that their allies joined them. Asked what was responsible for their not keeping the assignation, they said, 'Did you not tell us to come with a cuckoo when we came?' Nweke's people thereupon burst out laughing, and, up to the present time, they ridicule the people of this neighbouring town for their behaviour on this occasion.

At this stage, Nweke's training in village life ended. Very abruptly he was taken out of the village, to live in a society in close contact with Western Culture. It was the coming of the white man which brought radical changes into the village. We shall now see how he came and what changes followed.

6. The Coming of the White Man

THE WHITE MAN AT AWKA

In 1856 the Missionaries arrived at Onitsha, and the Government followed later. The Missionaries moved inland and reached Awka town about 1900. But a dispute broke out between two villages of Awka town, Amikwo-Awka and Agulu-Awka, and this grew to civil war between the two villages. The Missionaries did their very best to get the situation under control, but the people continued the war. The Missionaries, therefore, had no alternative but to seek the assistance of the white man at Onitsha, that is, the Government. The white man sent out his soldiers, whose weapons brought peace in Awka. This was the white man's first settlement in this district, and, using it as a base, he visited the surrounding towns and subjected them to his control.

THE WHITE MAN HEARD OF IN NWEKE'S VILLAGE

The news of the activities of the white man in other towns filtered into Nweke's village. One morning a sturdy youth, who had been out of the village early, was soon running back excited and alarmed. From a good distance off, he called to an elder and this dialogue took place.

69

The Coming of the White Man

Young man: Do you hear the latest news?

Elder: What is it?

Young man: We have just heard that 'the white man' is coming to our town.

Elder: To our town? Ha! Is that so? I believe it must be those beings who went to Awka. We have heard of how they fought the Awka people and defeated them.

Young man: Pay no attention to that. Those towns have always been weaklings. You remember how we treated them on various occasions, for which they now fear us.

Elder: Yes. This white man, no doubt, thinks that because he defeated those people, he could make us submit.

Young man: But from what land is this white man?

Elder: I do not know, but let him come! You know, this is an opportunity for us to capture white slaves. We!—the conquerors of the Ada!

Young man: You have spoken well. I am going to get ready my gun for them. This time they will learn a lesson.

The news ran round the village and, later, the Senior Man summoned a meeting of all the men. Many forceful speeches, expressing confidence and preparedness to challenge the white man when he came, were made. At the end of the meeting the senior man made a brief speech recalling their past victories in war, and he requested the people to provide enough gunpowder, and to keep their guns, knives, spears and other war instruments in good trim. The arrangement for the evacuation of women and children was postponed till another meeting. They had no idea when the white man

70

would come, and, though they determined to remain on their guard, they believed that the white man would give them further warning before he arrived.

VILLAGE SQUARE ENTERTAINMENT

A few days later the village held the festival of Oye Nemkpa, when people made sacrifices at the Nemkpa shrine, and dancing and masquerades were held in the village squares. About noon, a special dance organized by an age grade of young men was exhibited. It was a skilful performance and proved highly entertaining to a large crowd of men, women, boys and girls, who sat or stood around.

Suddenly a thundering blast sounded through the air. Everyone was astonished. All the performances stopped. No one knew what the noise was. Somebody, however, suggested at last that it was, perhaps, the white man's big gun, which he had heard spoken of. A hot debate broke out. Some said the white man could not have come so soon; others agreed that the noise could only have come from some special weapon. Then, again, the same terrific sound was heard twice in succession, nearer to the village. No further proof of the theory that the white man was on his way was required. The men, who had no idea of the power of the white man's gun, were determined to present a good defence. Meanwhile, the festivity came to an abrupt end and women and children hurriedly dispersed.

NWEKE'S VILLAGERS AND THE WHITE MAN

While the men consulted each other to determine in what direction to look for the white man, some people, who had been out of the village and had happened to see the effect of the white man's gun, rushed back and announced to the crowds that the white man's force was tremendous. They narrated how they had seen a gun-shot strike a tree and split it into pieces. They added that the white man was still advancing.

The people listened carefully to this report, since it came from some able warriors. Before anything else could be said, the white man fired his big gun again. The war commanders had a hurried conference and ordered the women and children to take refuge outside the village. The men, armed, took their watch points and were determined to fight and, if necessary, die, in defence of their village.

NWEKE RAN WITH HIS SENIOR BROTHER

Nweke was about seven years of age. He did not need to be carried or dragged by the hand, but ran himself on the first day. He and his elder brother hid themselves in the surrounding bushes. On the second day they took refuge in a neighbouring town, Nise. They returned home only when they heard that the white man had made peace with their people.

OTHER VILLAGES AND THE WHITE MAN

A number of villages (Ire, Urualo and Uruogbo) lay along the path by which the white man advanced, and the people of these villages made an attempt to resist him.

They, too, were enjoying their festival entertainments in the village square and were taken by surprise. Shortly after they became aware of the approach of the white man, a defence operation was organized. Women and children sought for hiding-places and the men, armed, took their watch positions. Further news of the white man's approach was signalled by a man who had climbed to the top of a tall tree to watch his movements. When the war signaller announced the continued advance, a single threatening gun-shot was fired by a villager in the direction of the enemy. This was intended as a warning to the white man and his army, who became more cautious in their approach.

But the soldiers heard the sound of the signaller's gong strokes high up in the air, and, after keen observation, they located his position in a tree and shot at him. The bullet hit the tree, which was split into pieces. When the people saw this, they were terribly alarmed. It was a mystery to them. They soon realized the strength of the white man. Meanwhile, the army fired threatening shots, whose terrible thundering sound compelled the people to retreat.

THE WHITE MAN'S ARMY

About two hundred Africans in hats, shorts, puttees and red tunic coats, buttoned to the waist, their brazen guns shining under the tropical sun—these were the soldiers of the white man.

In the rear followed the carriers, whose only duty was to carry the loads. The white man, who was the Commander, was carried in a hammock. People said he had no toes, and rightly so, for he wore shoes.

THE WHITE MAN OCCUPIED NWEKE'S TOWN

The white man and his army advanced slowly, without opposition. They arrived at the Nkwọ market, which is the principal market of the town, but could find nobody there. For all the men lay concealed waiting for an opportunity to demonstrate their superior military skill. On the evening of the same day the soldiers started to search the compounds surrounding the market, but could find no one. Later, some of the war commanders—men of sturdy physique, men of courage, men of wit—who lay concealed and watched the white man and his army, voluntarily came out, armed, to meet them. There could be no doubt that they had intelligently summarized the situation. The white man encouraged them to come to him by gestures, and through an interpreter assured them that he had not come to fight, and asked them to call back their comrades. After much persuasion, these men undertook to announce that the fight had ended, and that the white man was prepared to make peace. More men gradually came out. Eventually a large crowd assembled and the white man gently beckoned them to come nearer to him.

As they stood before him, a soldier fired a shot at a tree. The bullet split the stem of the tree into pieces. This demonstration was presumably meant to frighten the people and make them accept what the white man had to say. He addressed them through an interpreter, saying again that it was not his intention to fight. He then asked them whether they would attack him, and they said they would not. To make sure that the men were serious in this declaration, he requested them to build a temporary house for him and to provide food for his soldiers. These things they agreed to do. The following day they provided water and food for the soldiers, and built a temporary house for the white man, thereby endorsing their unconditional surrender. He ordered them to bring their guns, which he burnt to ashes. The iron parts he buried by the borders of the market, and they were rediscovered in 1915, when the C.M.S. Church members were collecting mud from a hollow for their Church building.

The Coming of the White Man

THE SOLDIERS BURNT NWEKE'S VILLAGE

After peace was made, the soldiers became undisciplined and began to plunder and burn people's houses. These outrageous acts by the servants of the white man made the people distrust and hate him, for though the white man may not have been a party to these misdeeds, anything done by his soldiers was regarded as his design.

Thus, the first impression of the people was that the white man was somebody without human feelings, a cruel being, and accurst of Ana the earth deity. Hence they grew very suspicious of his actions and preferred to avoid him and his agents as much as they could.

This feeling was intensified when the hated system of Native Administration was introduced. This Administration was conducted through the so-called Native Courts, which were artificially created and whose members, the 'Warrant Chiefs', were regarded as henchmen or stooges of the white man rather than as the spokesmen or leaders of the people. I shall return to this topic later.

WHY NWEKE'S PEOPLE OPPOSED THE WHITE MAN

It should be made clear that it was not out of mere hatred that Nweke's people opposed the white man. In doing this, they were only expressing their natural independence, which was found in all their institutions. Every family, every extended family or group of relatives, every village and village-group, managed its own affairs and tolerated no unnecessary outside interference. Though there were occasions when activities were communal, there was a strong individualistic tendency in all institutions.

75

The Coming of the White Man

According to official records, the white man came to Nweke's town in 1905. Those men who saw the white man come, and who were my informants, could only say that he came one Oye day when they had the Nemkpa festival, and that this was shortly after the civil war between Amikwo-Awka and Agulu-Awka. Everyone was illiterate, so no written records were kept in the village.

7. Christian Supporters and Christian Converts

The white man had come to stay. This was the transition period—a period of intense conflict between Indigenous Culture and Western Culture. The old was dying and the new was being born. Men experienced the changes with mixed feelings.

In Nweke's village, a man called Okonkwọ Ezeunọ was the pioneer of the new age. He was over eighty years of age when he died in 1956. He told me his story. In his teens, he was the epitome of valour and strength. He was feared and respected for his prowess by his fellows. The senior grades of men admired his keenly adventurous spirit, his charm and his wisdom.

When the white man and his soldiers arrived in the town, he took particular interest in watching them and in associating with them. He wanted to know where they came from and how they lived. When they visited the town again, he followed them back to Awka. There he gladly took up employment with the white man as a carrier. His main duty was to travel to Onitsha, a distance of about twenty-two miles, carrying on his head the soldiers' loads. He was highly pleased with the new contacts he had made, and would have liked to learn the white man's language, though the nature of his work did not give him the opportunity to do so.

Christian Supporters and Christian Converts

By this time, the white man had recruited court clerks, court messengers and police, and these men were held in high regard. Since they were backed by the power of the white man, their opinions were considered by the people indisputable and final. Any menial worker who gained the favour of one of these superior persons felt protected, since he could appeal to his patron to intervene if he were ever maltreated by another worker. Ezeuno wanted to gain this protection; he also wanted to find somebody who could study the white man and his men, and could pass on to him any information he gained about them. Ezeuno, therefore, associated with Mr. Onwuzuligbo, a Police Constable and a native of Amawbia town. Mr. Onwuzuligbo was highly respected in his office and had great influence over the other workers. To earn his favour, Ezeuno promised to send him his 'brother' to be his personal servant.

Nweke Left the Village

It was Nweke whom Ezeuno had in mind when he made this promise to Mr. Onwuzuligbo.

Nweke had already proved the most helpful of all of Ezeuno's young relatives, and Ezeuno was therefore confident that Nweke would improve, not harm, the good relations between Mr. Onwuzuligbo and himself. When next he went home he accordingly asked Nweke whether he would like to go to Amawbia, and Nweke readily gave his assent. Indeed, he was overjoyed at the scheme, but Ezeuno warned him not to mention it to anyone. Association with the white man was still regarded as improper, and if Nweke's mother had learnt of the proposal, she would certainly have forbidden him to leave the village. Her objection would have been that, once away from the village, he might be sold into slavery. Hence, one early morning, Ezeuno slipped out of the village with Nweke and handed him over to Mr. Onwuzuligbo to serve him. This was in the year 1910 and Nweke was twelve years of age.

At Amawbia, Nweke found himself in a strange society. The Government servants and their families dressed in a different fashion and lived in quite a different way from that in his village. But he soon adapted himself to the new environment, and picked up a few words of the English language.

Nweke Goes to School

It was a big day for Nweke when, dressed in a short loin-cloth, he was sent to school for the first time. He was the first person from his village to attend school. He was exceedingly happy at this change in his life, and worked hard both at home and at school.

His first school was a mud-walled rectangular building with a thatched roof, built by the Church Missionary Society. The school hours were from 1 p.m. to 4 p.m. The top class then was Infants II. The children were taught Reading, Writing, Spelling, Arithmetic, English and Bible Study. Nweke was good at his school work. He also attended Sunday Services and the Sunday Bible Class.

Nweke's Mother Accuses Ezeuno

The friction between Ezeuno and Nweke's mother, which arose out of his taking away her son to Amawbia, clearly illustrates the fate of the early sponsors of Western Civilization. Like Ezeuno, they were called all sorts of names and were highly unpopular.

A few hours after Ezeuno had left with Nweke, his mother

learnt of it. Fury seized her, and, if Ezeuno had appeared before her then, there is no doubt that she would have done him great harm. She told her story to the elders, some of whom, however, had known of Ezeuno's plan. They had not seen the sense in taking such a small boy away from the village, but out of their respect for Ezeuno they had allowed him to have his own way. Now, to comfort the child's mother, they assured her that her son was safe in the hands of Ezeuno.

But, in the village, the news was spread that Nweke had been taken away to be trained as a soldier, and would never return. Some people even suggested that he had been sold into slavery. The women, in particular, kept asking Nweke's mother why she had permitted her child to be taken away from her, and they pointed out the danger to the child if he associated with the white man. Although the mother did all she could, neither Ezeuno nor Nweke could be found.

When at length Ezeuno paid a visit to the village, he received a violent scolding from Nweke's mother. She demanded her child back, and openly accused him of selling Nweke into slavery. He did all he could to assure her that her child was safe, but she was unconvinced. He, however, was satisfied with his action and was unmoved by her pleas.

Unfortunately, Nweke fell seriously ill while at Amawbia, and at one time there was little hope that he would survive. When his mother heard this, she naturally concluded that it was Ezeuno's intention to kill her child, and she henceforth regarded him as her greatest enemy. People began to wonder whether Ezeuno was really acting in good faith. Had Nweke remained in the village, they said, he would not have contracted such an illness.

These accusations began to alarm Ezeuno, and he thought seriously of bringing Nweke back. But he found it difficult to ask Mr. Onwuzuligbo to release him, since his treatment of the child was good. However, Nweke at last recovered completely from the illness, and Ezeuno, therefore, with the permission of his patron, took him home, where he was received like a lost lamb.

Contrary to the expectation of the villagers, he was more robust and handsome than when he left. They were forced to agree that he must have been treated well. But they also argued that this meant that he had not been working hard, and they absurdly concluded that he lived a lazy life with the white man.

NWEKE BACK TO AMAWBIA

Everybody thought Nweke had returned home for good, but one day, not long after his return, he expressed the desire to go back to his guardian. His mother once more grew alarmed. She did all she could to dissuade him from leaving the village again, and other members of his kindred did the same. But he cheerfully bade them good-bye and left again for Amawbia.

His mother believed he was doing the wrong thing and continued to accuse Ezeuno of being responsible for the change in the attitude of her son. In the village both Nweke and Ezeuno were talked about unfavourably.

That Nweke, young as he was and without support from anyone, was able to disregard the attempts of his mother and other members of his kindred to turn him aside from the road to success he had discovered, shows his independence of mind and strength of will.

NWEKE RETURNS TO LIVE IN THE VILLAGE

Nweke continued to live with his guardian at Amawbia. But, after several more months, Ezeuno was so disturbed by the attitude of the villagers towards himself that he advised Nweke to return to his mother, and his guardian gave Nweke the same advice. Nweke returned to his village in the year 1912, during his school holidays. His mother and his kindred welcomed him back with great joy.

However, his experiences when he returned as a Christian illustrate the difficulties of the early Christian convert. Shortly after his return a village festival was held. All the children had smiles on their faces, for much meat and other food was being prepared for them to eat. As part of the festival, fowls were killed at the village shrine. Nweke, like other boys, was called on to take part in the ritual, but he declined to do so. When he found the pressure from his mother and elders was becoming too great, he went away unnoticed. When it was time to consume the food he was nowhere to be found, and not till the feast was over did he return. Questioned as to his whereabouts, he said not a word. This was the first public demonstration of the effect of Christian belief on him. His mother and other relatives were worried about this behaviour, but concluded that it was because of laziness that he did not take part in the preparation of the food. They could not understand why he did not want to share in the feast.

But they soon found he was no longer a member of their society. He refused to eat anything—fowl, goat or cow—killed on the shrine. He would not take part in any sacrificial proceeding either in the family or in the village. He refrained from the use of camwood. He gave no attention to village dances. Other young men were always interested in masquerading, but he dissociated himself from their society. He was seen cutting sticks from taboo bushes. Before he left the village he had not behaved like this; in fact, he had been a leader in these activities. Yet, although he would have nothing to do with ceremonies, he did not fail in his domestic duties and his duties in the village. For instance, he worked hard on the farm for the greater part of the day.

However, his attitude of indifference towards village affairs was noted by all in the village and invariably he became the subject of much gossip. His mother regarded him as a spoilt boy and only tolerated him because he was hard-working. And then, when the holidays were over, he went back to school.

The school was about four miles from his home and he trudged this distance daily along winding paths (there were no motor roads then). The school hours were 1 p.m. to 4 p.m. and he therefore got up early in the morning to do his share of work in the compound and on the farm. He watched the sun to find out the time, and when it was nearly overhead he prepared to leave and go to school. It was then that his mother grew angry with him. Though he had done a good share of the work, she would not concede him the privilege of leaving the farm, for she did not consider anything more important than farm work. In her view he was a very badly behaved youth.

Eventually she made up her mind not to provide food for him before he went to school, and when he returned she scolded him, saying, 'Yes, you have gone to learn to be lazy, and now that you are back you expect your servant to toil and get food ready for you. You think you know better than the other youths who remain at home? Come and eat now, you foolish boy.' Sometimes he was given no food on his return and went to bed hungry. He was so resolute in his course that he did not even trouble to ask any member of his kindred for food.

His father's second wife observed that he went hungry several times and had compassion on him. One day she called

83

him to her and fed him. Ever after, she provided food for him, and gave him maternal care. His mother, who adopted strict disciplinary measures to dissuade him, was astonished when she observed that he was not in the least worried. With the little money he earned by selling roof mats he had made himself, Nweke was able to buy food at the market on the days he went to school. This was his first difficulty as a Christian convert.

He was lucky that, despite the disagreement between his mother and himself, he was allowed to remain peacefully in the compound. Many young Christian converts of his time suffered very cruel treatment from their parents, and often they were compelled to run away to live somewhere else. Some parents deliberately drove their children away because they went to school. Although the majority of parents behaved badly towards those of their children who went to school, there were a small number who tolerated them. One woman, Nwamgbeke Uzuagu of Umuọkpaleri, was especially kind to these children. Although she never became a Christian (she died in 1948, an old woman), her home was the rendezvous for many schoolchildren, and those driven away by their parents lived with her. Because of her association with these children and her interest in their affairs, she attended and contributed to the Church Harvest Festival, though she was not a Christian.

The peculiar characteristic of these early young Christian converts was their fearlessness. They did not hesitate to speak their minds in objection to anything—particularly the indigenous ceremonies. They were taught that any indigenous ceremony was the work of the devil and should not be encouraged. Wherever the Christians lived, one, two or more, they expressed this view and defied the reactions of the non-Christians. The latter often rebuked them, but sometimes

84

they did not take them seriously and scoffed at them. Nweke at this period had no companion and was alone in his village with his 'strange' doctrine.

WRESTLING EARNED HIM RESPECT

Wrestling was an important sport in all villages. There were seasonal contests between age-grades, and elaborate preparations were made for these occasions.

In Nweke's village this sport was regarded as a test of strength between individuals and between age-grades. There were senior and junior wrestling contests. The arrangement was such that every age-grade took part in the wrestling contest twice: first in the junior group, and the following year in the senior group. Each of the two contesting age-grades selected their best wrestlers and gave them special coaching. A few weeks before the contest day they were smeared with camwood and placed on a special diet. The age-grades had their supporters, who urged on their favourite and wagered palm wine and other goods on the result of the contests. Thus the wrestling contests provided one of the most interesting spectacles in village life.

The contest day was a holiday for everyone. Long before the game started, the village square was packed full of people, including visitors from other villages. A special wrestling drum called Igba Mbe was played, and the music was an incentive to the wrestlers. When it was starting time, a contestant from the senior age-grade jumped into the square, ran around and challenged any contestant from the junior group. The sport had its rules and the elders were the umpires. The winning group, even if a junior group, lorded it for that season over all other groups. It was, however, disgraceful for a senior group to be defeated by a junior one.

Christian Supporters and Christian Converts

Nweke, as he grew up, became an excellent wrestler, and by his success in unofficial wrestling bouts proved himself well qualified to contest the issue on behalf of his age-grade. Yet, when it was his turn, because of his Christian beliefs, he refused to take part. The members of his age-grade were not a little hurt when they could not get him to contest for them.

Though the early Christian converts were greeted with offensive language wherever they went, Nweke did not tolerate insults from members of his age-grade or even from his seniors. He did not hesitate to challenge them to a private wrestling contest, in which he invariably knocked his opponent down.

Since it was humiliating to refuse such a challenge, the members of his age-grade were forced to swallow the abuse they had in store for him. In spite of his strange ideas he was respected, and old as well as young, both men and women, had a particular regard for him because of his wrestling ability.

NWEKE'S FIRST CHRISTIAN COMPANION

As footballers and boxers are admired by their fans, so Nweke was admired by some village children. Whenever he had the chance, he told these children about his new beliefs.

One day, one of them came to him and said that he would like to go to school with him. Nweke was delighted and congratulated the boy on his decision. To test his sincerity, he requested him to give him money to buy some school materials. In time, the boy was able to collect the sum of one shilling. This he handed to Nweke, who bought him a slate and other things required at school. On the slate Nweke wrote the alphabet for his new companion.

At the commencement of another school term, he took him

to school and introduced him to the schoolmaster. The master was amazed, since he had observed that Nweke's people were not interested in schooling. He congratulated Nweke and encouraged him to bring along more children from the village.

NWEKE WORKED FOR HIS MAINTENANCE

Nweke had now left his guardian and lived at home, and therefore had to pay his own school fees—which were, at first, one shilling a quarter. He also had to provide a few materials for his classwork. His clothing was in the first instance a loin-cloth, and later a pair of shorts. When he was in the upper classes, he added a singlet. He possessed only one of each of these articles and he used them until they were completely worn out. He had to do this because he was so poor. Such was the condition of the early pioneers of education in this village.

At home, his mother, who normally would still have cared for him, did not help him because he went to school. No other person in the village was prepared to give him financial aid. He was, therefore, forced to earn money to keep himself at school till he had completed his elementary education.

To do this, he made roof mats from palm tree leaves and sold them. He also cultivated a piece of land and sold the products. Because he was not allowed to farm on the family land, he cleared a portion of a taboo bush, commonly known as Ajọ Ọfia or 'Bad Bush', and farmed there.

THE AJỌ ỌFIA OR 'BAD BUSH'

The 'Bad Bush' was a stretch of land not far from the village which was regarded as the home of an evil spirit. The villagers threw into this bush all the things which they considered evil. No one owned the land and no one went near it. It was believed that anyone who cut down the trees there or removed anything from it would be chased by the evil spirit. But Christianity had taught Nweke to disregard such a belief.

His clearing the 'Bad Bush' caused great alarm in the village. People said, 'This boy appears not to care for anything. He now puts himself into the hands of the spirit, and will suffer the consequences.' Old men said, 'Our child, do you know what you are doing? Come out from there!' Nweke paid no attention, but cleared the bush and cultivated the land. The first harvest was very rich and he made a lot of money. Since no one questioned his right over the area, it became his personal property. Many early Christians did the same, and gained personal land by clearing portions of 'Bad Bush'. The villagers waited for Nweke to be attacked by an evil sickness, but instead he grew more robust and strong, and more capable of knocking down his opponents in wrestling contests.

He did not work much on the farm during the school session, but in the holidays spent all his time making the money to pay for the next quarter's schooling.

8. The Collapse of Local Institutions

Before the white man came, the administration of the villages was in the hands of the senior men. Most of these senior men held titles, so that it is correct to say that the administration and judicature of the village were in the hands of the titled men. But when the white man set up his first 'Native Court' in the town, these titled men were robbed of their traditional authority.

This 'Native Court', which was introduced by the white man not long after he took control of Nweke's town, had no relation to the existing forms of social life. The jurisdiction of this court covered a wide area of land containing previously unrelated social groups, so that it was difficult for the people to appreciate its significance. The Court was presided over by the white man, with a number of native members as his assessors. The appointment of these 'Native Court' members led to great trouble throughout Ibo land.

The traditional leaders of the people, though conscious of their responsibility in normal situations, failed to make any contact with the white man. This was because they generally behaved in a reserved way, and did not take the initiative in meeting people or in deciding matters. They waited for the white man to approach them.

But other men, who had no traditional authority, did not

89

hesitate to step forward. It was these men whom the white man appointed as members of the 'Native Court', the appointment being by a 'Warrant'. They took it in turn to sit on the bench with the white man, as his assessors. It was their duty to see that the orders of the white man were carried out in their respective village-groups. Because they usurped the functions of a chief, they were known as 'Warrant Chiefs', though they were merely agents of the white man, and bore no resemblance to true African Chiefs, who were fathers or spiritual heads of their people, and whose absolute powers were kept in constant check by means of taboos and councils.

On one occasion, one of these 'Warrant Chiefs' visited Nweke's village to announce that the white man wanted some men to carry his loads. Before the Warrant Chief had finished speaking, a senior titled man exclaimed, 'What is this boy thinking about? Does he not know where he is! I am going away.' Another remarked, 'Is that what he called us for? Do you think he is in his right senses?' Other senior men were equally annoyed, and said to the Warrant Chief, 'Is that what you have come to tell us—that we should come and carry loads! If the white man told you that, why did you not tell him we would not do it? Are we under any obligation to him?'

The Warrant Chief was not at all tactful, and when the villagers showed their resentment, he only made his orders more imperative. Still the people did not listen to him, so he threatened them, saying he was going to make them obey. He left, but soon returned, accompanied by two court messengers, who immediately arrested a senior titled man. The whole village was astir. But the villagers could do nothing, as they were by now fearful of the white man's war weapons. The Warrant Chief told them that the titled man would not be released until they had nominated the members of a party to carry the white man's loads. He departed with the arrested titled man, but before he had gone far he was called back, and the titled man was exchanged for a gang of young men, who were forced to carry the loads.

The arrest of this titled man was considered an insult and an abomination by the villagers, and their forced acceptance of the insult was humiliating. Titled men had previously always been considered as worthy of the highest respect. Thus the Warrant Chiefs earned nothing but hatred and disfavour in the village, and there were frequent clashes between them and the people. Had the white man first studied the social institutions of the people, and sent his orders through the traditional leaders, probably no hard feelings on the part of the people towards himself and his agents would have developed.

A little later, in order (he thought) to improve the standard of 'Native Administration', the white man retired from the presidency of the Native Court. His place was taken by Warrant Chiefs, and this gave them more opportunity for corrupt conduct, particularly as there was then no right of appeal from the 'Native Court'. These courts became the sole link between the white man and the people. Semi-educated Court Clerks, assisted by court messengers, took control of them. Both clerks and messengers were corrupt. They issued summonses, gave orders for arrest, and took custody of prisoners without consulting either the Warrant Chiefs or the white man. Because most of the Warrant Chiefs were illiterate, the Court Clerk was responsible for conveying the white man's orders to them, and this made his position very strong. There were many instances of Court Clerks issuing warrants of arrest against their personal enemies, and they, as well as the Warrant Chiefs, took large bribes.

Yet it must also be said that Warrant Chiefs at times gave protection to Christian converts, and they supported the

The Collapse of Local Institutions

schools by backing the Christians against their opponents. (On the other hand, at other times the Warrant Chiefs quarrelled with the literate Christians because they challenged the Chiefs' authority, and they then drove the Christians out of the town.) When the villagers saw that the power of the white man was too much for them, they adopted an attitude of indifference with regard to the schools and they obeyed, though with reluctance, the orders of the Warrant Chiefs.

The loss of their authority by the traditional rulers, and the corrupt conduct of the Warrant Chiefs, led to a rapid disintegration of local institutions. This being so, the term 'Native Court' was obviously a misnomer.

The period of conflict between Indigenous Culture and Western Culture was coming to an end. Indigenous culture was giving way to Western culture.

9. The Coming of the Church

The opposition of Nweke's people to the white man's culture now relaxed, and the Missionaries found their way to the town.

The first Christian converts attended school and Church services at Amawbia, about four miles away. It became their burning desire to possess a Church and a School in their home town. Under the leadership of Nweke they interviewed the local Catechist, who gave them directions as to how they might achieve their desire. They further consulted some of the Warrant Chiefs of the town, who gave them support. And, finally, they decided to interview Archdeacon Basden when next he visited Amawbia. Archdeacon Basden was one of the early Christian Missionaries of the Church Missionary Society in this area and he enjoyed the respect and regard of the people. He lived at Onitsha and visited the surrounding Christian stations in turn.

When next he visited Amawbia, a delegation comprising a Warrant Chief and four Christians interviewed him. The Warrant Chief was the spokesman, while the Catechist interpreted. After hearing what they had to say, the Archdeacon replied that he would inquire further to find out if they expressed the wishes of their people correctly. If they did, he assured them that when next he visited a neighbouring town,

Nawfia, to dedicate a Church there, he would the same day settle the arrangements for Enugwu-Ukwu.

On this appointed day, after the dedication of the Church at Nawfia, the delegation met him again. He asked whether they had the support of the senior Warrant Chief. 'Yes,' was the reply. He then followed them to their town, where he was the senior Warrant Chief's guest. To the Archdeacon's question whether he supported the demand for a Church the senior Warrant Chief replied, 'As they want it, let them have it.' When the Archdeacon asked for land for Church premises, they showed him a piece of 'Bad Bush' known as Ugwu Nwifi —the present site of the church building of the Church Missionary Society.

Before the Archdeacon left, he gave orders that a Church building and a Catechist's house should be erected, and warned the people that their having a Church depended on how soon they completed the buildings. These were considered minor conditions by the Christians. They were exceedingly joyful about the success of their appeal to the Archdeacon. Immediately, they summoned a meeting, contributed money and arranged to proceed with the work.

When some of the Christians who were natives of Enugwu-Ukwu, but who lived elsewhere, learnt of the proposal to build a Church in their home town, they were filled with joy and returned to join in the work. Both labour and building materials were provided voluntarily and the work commenced in earnest. This was in 1913, and the next year the Church was dedicated. In 1915, the first class of the infant primary school was started. The building of a Church gave an opportunity for an organized membership drive, and the Christian community grew quickly. The maintenance and growth of the Church was the direct responsibility of these Christians. Serious evangelization commenced, and on Sunday evenings

The Coming of the Church

Church members paraded the villages, under the direction of the Catechist, who preached the gospel.

Nweke, now sixteen years of age, attended school at Amawbia, but on Sundays it gave him great pleasure to attend the Church at his home.

Christian education plunged these pioneers further into western culture. With their increased knowledge, they observed the despotic authority of the Warrant Chiefs, and soon a graver antagonism broke out between the Warrant Chiefs and the scholars than the previous one between the Warrant Chiefs and the illiterates.

THE WARRANT CHIEF'S TRESPASS

At about this time a Warrant Chief, who was not a member of Nweke's village and had no claim to anything therein, without consultation with the villagers or their permission, cleared a good portion of the village land to cultivate. Nweke was infuriated at the domineering attitude of this Warrant Chief, and resolved to prevent this trespass. In the company of another Christian, he approached a certain powerful Court Messenger and implored him to dissuade the Warrant Chief from taking the land. They took to the Court Messenger the usual presents of a cock, some yams and some wine, in return for which he assured them he would do his best to meet their wishes. The following day he sent for them again. Addressing them, he said, 'I have seen our man is very determined, but I am working hard to get him to appreciate our view.' He then demanded further presents, including a young maid-servant. They agreed to the other presents but objected to giving him a maid-servant. He persisted. There being no other alternative, they brought him his presents and the maid-servant. He then successfully influenced the Warrant Chief, who did not cultivate the land. Though Nweke and his colleagues were happy at their success, they lamented giving away their young relative to serve the Messenger.

The influence of Education and Christianity was now telling on Nweke. So, not long after, he called his village Christians and said, 'You know that we were not happy when we gave our sister to that man. I am still not satisfied with her remaining there. Should anything untoward happen to her, what will be our position? We had better do something to get her back.' Another member replied, 'Yes, these people have been demanding too much from us. We must get our sister away from that man, and if he worries us we will report him to the Archdeacon. But the problem is, how can we get her back?' Nweke replied, 'Wait, we will be very tactful about it. We will go to greet him with presents of yam and wine. When we are about to leave, we will beg him to allow our sister to come and enjoy the forthcoming feast with us and, at the same time, assure him we will unfailingly send her back after the festival. He does not know our plan and he will not refuse. When she comes, we will not allow her to go back.' His second replied, 'That is a good suggestion. If he makes any trouble we shall know what to do.' They followed Nweke's suggestion and brought the girl back to the village.

The Court Messenger, when his maid-servant failed to come back, sent a message to Nweke's village, threatening that if she was not sent back he would create trouble for the villagers. But no reply was returned. He therefore went himself. When he asked, 'Did you not receive my message?' Nweke said, 'Yes, we would have sent her to you, but according to Church law it would be wrong to do so. You know she is not your wife; but if you still want her, let us go to the Archdeacon and tell him.' Here the Messenger frowned and said, 'You boys, you want to show that you are becoming wise? All right, you will see!' Very unceremoniously, he walked away. Another Church member then added, 'Oh, so he is afraid of the Archdeacon! When the Archdeacon comes again we will tell him that this man is coming to worry us.' The boys expected to be arrested the following day, but nothing happened. So from this period they began to learn how to check the despotic powers of these petty tyrants.

We shall now see what happened to these scholars when they defended their rights.

There was still some goodwill between the scholars and the Warrant Chiefs while Nweke was in the village, but he had left by the time the relationship became acutely strained and the Warrant Chiefs tried to suppress the revolution which he started. Any scholar who would not obey their orders was severely punished. Such punishment was in the nature of hard labour on the Warrant Chief's farm or on the public road under construction. Some of the scholars were said to have been arrested and imprisoned without trial.

In the course of my inquiry, a member of the Roman Catholic Church gave an account of a grim experience in his life at this time—an incident which contributed to the rapid growth of the Church. Because I doubted his story, he referred me to another person who was also a member of the Roman Catholic Church and demanded, 'Go to him to confirm my story. He was the most intelligent of us at that time; perhaps he will give you more details than I have done.'

So I went to see this man who, I think, was in his early fifties. I had a cordial welcome and he offered me sweet palm wine, which I enjoyed. Soon we were talking, and I put my question: 'I was told that you were one of those who were arrested and locked up in a small room by a Warrant Chief, but were released on the intervention of the Reverend Father. Would you please tell me the story all over again. I find it difficult to believe that such an arrest did take place.' 'It did, my young man,' he quickly cut in, and continued, 'Before that, I had been to prison. For four days I was at Awka cutting grass with other prisoners. It happened like this. One morning, I was walking by the Court premises when someone hailed me. It was a Warrant Chief and I went to him. He ordered me to go to his farm and join other workers there. I refused. He then held my two hands and pulled me towards the Court building. I struggled with him until a Court Messenger came along and both of them overpowered me. I was handcuffed and taken to Awka by the Court Messenger. Before this incident, however, there had been some unpleasantness between us.'

I interrupted him with another question. 'On what grounds did the Court find you guilty and send you to prison?' 'Court?' he ejaculated, 'Nothing like that. I was taken there and locked up in a small room. Later, I was taken out to join other prisoners to cut grass. Sometimes the man who was in charge would say I was not working hard enough, and would give me some strokes on my back with his long whip. My food was dried cassava and kernel. I drank water only when we went to the stream to have a bath or fetch water for use in the Prison. I was taken back to my small room after the day's work. I was glad when I was allowed to go home. The hardship was more than I could endure and so, in future, I obeyed, though reluctantly, all orders of the Warrant Chief. A few others had a similar experience.'

There was a brief pause, and he continued, 'Now to your question. If those Warrant Chiefs had had their way they would have destroyed all of us. They found that because we went to school we learnt to oppose them. This Warrant Chief who sent me to Awka, therefore, hatched a plan to stop us from going to school. Some of us, who, he thought, were very stubborn and perhaps the leaders of the scholars, were ordered to join the labourers in road work then in progress. We dared not say a word of protest, knowing the consequence would be bitter for us. So, every day, instead of going to school we went to work on the road.

'When the Reverend Father did not see us in the school for some days, he came to us to find out why we had stopped our schooling. We told him we wanted to go to school but the Warrant Chief would not allow us. We told him how we worked on the road. He was very angry about this. It was not our duty, he said, to work on the road and, should the Warrant Chief send us there again, we should let him know immediately. He urged us to go to school the following day. We went, but on our return home we were arrested by the Warrant Chief. Eight of us were locked up in a small room in a building in the Court premises. In this small and stuffy room we spent the night. At dawn, we were exhausted and almost suffocated. When at noon we were released, I was very weak and just managed to walk home.

'Later, I was told that the news of our arrest was communicated to the Reverend Father the following morning. He rode on his bicycle to the Court Clerk and asked for the reason for the arrest, but he denied knowledge of it. The Reverend Father then went to the white man (District Officer) at Awka, who described the arrest as improper and ordered our release.

'The Court Clerk quickly informed the Warrant Chief of what was happening. The Warrant Chief sought his cooperation to save his face. "They must be released," the Court Clerk replied, "Father said they are his children. He has gone to Awka and the white man will be against us." While they were still arguing, orders came that we should be released. The news of this arrest was a stunning shock to the people. But what could they do? Nothing! When they learnt that it was the Reverend Father who saved us, they acknowledged his action with a deep sense of gratitude. The Reverend Father now gave us positive protection. Many young men who had been sceptical about Christianity now found security in the Church, and came to register in our Church. The Church quickly grew and became strong. This action of the Reverend Father was one of the reasons why the Roman Catholic Church members quickly outnumbered those of the C.M.S., in spite of the fact that the latter came to the village-group first.'

10. Denominational Strife

In 1919, the influence of the Roman Catholic Mission reached the town. With the support of certain persons, the Reverend Father started to erect a Church building at Umuakwu village in the town. Because their permission was not sought before the building was commenced, the Warrant Chiefs encouraged the villagers to oppose the Mission and to demolish the building. In the course of a little fracas which occurred while the Church building was being knocked down, the Warrant Chiefs arrested and imprisoned some of the people connected with the new Mission. The persecution was so intense that the Reverend Father had to move to a neighbouring town, Nimo.

The Catholic converts in Nweke's town had to trudge to Nimo for Church services and for school until 1921, when they established a Church in the town without opposition.

Because the C.M.S. Church had come to stay in Nweke's town, the members expected other people to join and support it. They were, therefore, disappointed when some of the people started to build another Church.

The Catholics were convinced that they were the only one, and the only true, and the only acceptable Church of God. They therefore looked down upon and despised the C.M.S. members as unworthy to associate with them.

This basic outlook engendered an intolerable spirit of hatred and antagonism between the Catholics on one side and the C.M.S. members on the other. And so it happened that no matter how close the blood relationship, members of the two Churches seldom associated with each other.

There were many instances of fighting in public between the members of these two Churches, arising out of their religious differences.

Neither R.C.M. nor C.M.S. members attended the functions of the other body. A member of either considered it unworthy to give assistance to a member of the other. They could not meet on a common platform to discuss any matter affecting the general welfare of the town. There was antagonism and discrimination everywhere. The Christians did not agree with the non-Christians, and among themselves there was no co-operation. All this brought about the complete collapse of the indigenous institutions directing community development, and any progress was only in the direction of the aping of the white man's culture.

How Nweke Bridged the Gulf

This state of affairs continued till the year 1941, when a dramatic change occurred. I will now show how this change came about, but will continue the story of Nweke's early life in the next chapter.

By this time, many people had left the town and sought a career elsewhere, as traders, or servants of the white man. These people gained wealth and education, so that, when they returned home, they stood out above those who had remained in the village. Nweke was one of those. He worked for the white man, and increased his wealth and influence, and his patronage was sought in all aspects of community life.

Denominational Strife

My father worked in the Post Office but, strangely enough, when he wrote letters he seldom took them to the post-box himself. I was usually the postman. My mother once complained, 'Why send him all that way when you are going there yourself?' My father explained that he often forgot to post them when he took them away himself. This was because he was confronted with office work immediately on arrival at the Post Office, and consequently he forgot his private business.

Some of the letters I took to the post in 1941 were addressed to a prominent member of the R.C.M. in Enugwu-Ukwu. The contents I did not know then. But later, among my father's papers, I read replies from this gentleman. The denominational strife between the R.C.M. and C.M.S. Church members was the subject of their correspondence.

In his earlier letters, this R.C.M. member justified the R.C.M. attitude and argued that it was the rule of the Church. In one of his later letters, he said, *inter alia*, 'I agree . . . but I cannot change the rule.'

The seed of unity was sown then, but as yet the soil was unfavourable for its growth.

A change came in December 1941, when my father returned home on leave. The R.C.M. members had learnt a new dance called Etiliogwu, which they wished to perform at Christmas and at the New Year, and were looking for a Patron to honour their dance. There was no influential person better fitted for this than my father, and therefore, though they doubted whether he would agree, they came to him and asked him to be their Patron.

The R.C.M. member had visited my father, and I believe his influence affected whatever transpired on the R.C.M. side at that time.

It was a cold, dry, *harmattan* morning. My father had gone out early to see his sister in a neighbouring village. I was sweeping the ground in front of our house—very brisk sweeping I did to keep warm. A stranger suddenly appeared. 'Is your father in?' he asked. 'No,' I replied. 'Can I see your mother? I have a message for your father.'

I took him to my mother, who was busy in the kitchen. He told her that he was sent by the R.C.M. Dance Committee to inform my father that the Committee would visit him in the evening to discuss an important matter.

About an hour after this message came my mother called me and asked, 'Did your father say when we should expect him?' 'By noon,' I replied. She continued, 'I think it is best I communicate this message to him immediately. I am not aware he has any business with these R.C.M. people.'

My father got the message, and hurried back before noon. He summoned one of the best palm wine tappers in the village, and ordered two gallons of undiluted palm wine. He hurried back so as to get this order through, to ensure the evening supply of a wine which was very much in demand.

My mother consulted him to learn what guests she should expect. 'What is it they are coming to discuss with you?' she asked. 'I haven't the slightest idea,' he replied.

At dusk, five men stood at the front door of our house. 'Are you from the R.C.M.?' I asked. 'Yes,' was the reply. I ushered them into the sitting-room. None of the faces was familiar to me. My father appeared, and soon the business of the evening was well under way amidst his characteristic hospitality. I served palm wine. The spokesman started with a preamble, and concluded, 'We have a dance which we intend to put on at Christmas and at the New Year, and we have come to ask you to be our Patron.' 'What!' my father exclaimed laughingly, looking each of them in the face, 'is that a decision of your Church Committee?' 'We are the Dance Committee. The Church Committee has nothing to do in this matter,' was their reply. There was a brief silence, and my father looked a bit thoughtful. 'I have no objection,' he replied, 'I will do it with pleasure. Let me know the time you decide to arrive at my compound, and any other arrangements which concern me.'

His brief silence was out of wonder at the unexpected request and its implications—the R.C.M. recognizing a C.M.S. personality! He must have also recognized that a pressure group in favour of a change of outlook must exist, and felt that it was worth while to encourage them.

His reply was reported to the dancing party, who were delighted to hear it. Soon afterwards, the news spread. The members of the C.M.S. became alarmed when they learnt of his patronage of the R.C.M. dancers, and some of them attempted to persuade him to withdraw his acceptance. They argued that the dancers were only attracted by his social position, and, in view of their past attitude towards them, they should not be allowed to make use of his name. But he refused to listen, and, instead, launched a campaign among the leaders of the C.M.S. to make them understand that an opportunity had come for them all to demonstrate to the R.C.M. members the need for co-operation in the town.

His attitude was not new, for he had endeavoured previously—by letters when away from home and by personal contacts on occasional visits—to infuse this spirit of co-operation into the intelligent members of the town Churches.

He made a grand preparation for this particular occasion. On the eve of the exhibition day, the party, in their colourful costumes, danced gracefully into our compound. Suddenly the drum rhythm changed—it became much faster. The 'talking drum' was in the hands of a tall, handsome young man. He propped it between his knees and did his 'talking'— a marvellous performance indeed. He was 'talking' to the dance leader, a smart, well-built boy of about sixteen. He understood, and swiftly dashed forward about ten yards away from the others. There he started dancing, on his left foot, and ending with intricate variations of dancing and acrobatics. He drew applause. My father, clean-shaven, looking smart and superbly stately in his expensive traditional costume, stepped out of his house and walked towards the dancer. I saw him pulsating with the rhythm. With dignity, he adjusted his costume, then threw his right foot forward; then the left. I said to myself, 'What is he going to do?' and stared. Next he made a sweeping gesture with his hands, and started dancing. Tremendous applause followed. I was much excited. I looked around. Mamma was not there to enjoy the fun with me. I ran to the kitchen. 'Mamma, Mamma, come and see Papa dancing, come, come!' That was the first and only time I saw my father dance. He danced with simplicity and dignity, and finally embraced the young dance leader. He said the drumming should continue. His well-prized double-barrelled gun was soon brought out, and he fired several shots. This was symbolic of a special honour. The drumming stopped. The solo dancing and embracing were the traditional expression of mutual respect and goodwill. That was the end of the first scene of this great occasion.

There was food and drink in plenty. I remember that no palm wine producer in the village sold his produce out of the village that day. I heard a special public announcement to this effect four days earlier. Till late in the night, dancing went on with much jubilation.

It was a night to remember. A night, a villager said, when the white man had made 'moon', for my father had bought three 500-candle-power gas-lamps, which lit the scene with a brilliance I never saw before.

Among his presents to the guests were a cow and some

goats, which they were surprised to receive. The provision of a cow became a precedent for future occasions. My father's generous gesture and his benevolence impressed themselves deeply on the hearts of all in the town, Christians and non-Christians alike. This was the initial move in the reconciliation of the R.C.M. and the C.M.S. members.

His patronage on the exhibition day drew spectators from both Churches and from among the non-Christians, and he further honoured the dance by firing some shots from his double-barrelled gun. In the course of his opening speech, he emphasized the need for unity between the members of the two Churches. For the first time prayers were said in common, refreshment served in common, and they drank to the health of each other. There and then was planted the seed of reconciliation between the R.C.M. and C.M.S.

11. The Beginning of Mass Emigration

Nineteen hundred and eighteen was the year of the influenza epidemic, when hundreds of people in the villages died. This epidemic is remembered as a landmark in the history of the town.

The year after, Nweke was in his last class at school, Standard VI. He was the first person in his town to attain such a standard of education. This was the highest academic attainment in the whole locality at this time, and whoever reached it was much respected in Christian circles.

When he left school at twenty-one Nweke had opportunities for employment either as a teacher or as a clerk. In fact, people of his type were very much needed to man the posts in the white man's offices and schools. Nweke had no aptitude for teaching, and declined invitations to assume such posts. He had not yet decided to leave the village to take up a job, so he continued to labour for his maintenance. He collected his farm products and sold them at distant markets, where he made good profits. Shortly after the completion of his schooling, he travelled on foot to Onitsha (eighteen miles away) for the first time, in the company of some of his Christian friends. He carried a basket of oranges, which he hoped to sell at a good price. He was highly impressed by the various interesting features of Western life at Onitsha, and quickly decided to leave home.

Shortly after his return to his village he went to Awka, the local administrative headquarters, to inquire into the conditions for taking up a job under the white man. There and then he was selected to work as a postal clerk and telegraphist in the Posts and Telegraphs Department. He returned home, got ready, bade farewell to his relatives and friends, and left the village finally to take up the job. The villagers watched him leave with wonder and amazement.

He was soon transferred to Lagos, the capital of Nigeria, where he did his training in the school for telegraphists. His appointment dated as from the 26th June 1920. At a time when no one from his town had travelled as far as a hundred miles, Nweke travelled over four hundred miles to a town with a different language and culture. He was also the first person from Enugwu-Ukwu to take up regular employment in the white man's Civil Service. At Lagos, he found himself in the heart of western civilization, and soon lost every trace of his village upbringing.

The period 1919 to 1921 marked the beginning of a mass emigration from Nweke's town. School pupils who had completed their course (and some who had not) left the town. A few children were taken away by the Missionaries, to be trained and put into good jobs.

But the most important cause of emigration was a farm dispute which broke out in 1919.

THE AMAKOBAM ATROCITY

The people of Nweke's town originally practised subsistence farming within the town boundaries. But, as population increased and the productivity of the land decreased, there was need for more farming land in order to sustain life, and so the people were forced to look for land in places outside the town.

Many farmers made their way to a town called Igbariam, about ten miles away. This town owned a vast area of fertile land, much of it uncultivated by the town people. A good part was cultivated by seven neighbouring towns, who were known collectively as Amakọbam, meaning 'the Alliance'. These towns had been on this land for a number of years before Nweke's people applied to the landlords for land, and when Nweke's people were allowed to cultivate an area of land it was adjacent to the area cultivated by the towns mentioned.

Nweke's people grew excellent crops on this land, and, out of jealousy and spite, those towns who first occupied part of the land protested against Nweke's people being allowed there, and worked hard to eject them from the land. Now Nweke's people did not live permanently at their farms, but returned home after some days' work. At feasting times, in particular, no one remained on the farms. On one of these occasions, when all the farmers had gone home, the rival towns set fire to their houses and farms. There was nobody to put out the fire and all their possessions were destroyed. It was a brutal destruction of their wealth—a gross inhumanity to man.

News of this incident reached Nweke's people, and they hurried back to the farm. Very law-abiding as they were, they first asked their landlords for an explanation. The latter denied any connection with the act and condemned in unequivocal terms the action of the Amakọbam group. Further investigation proved conclusively that the Amakọbam group were the sole perpetrators of this act.

Here was another opportunity for Nweke's people to demonstrate their military valour. Accepting the challenge, they launched an attack on the Amakọbam towns and inflicted damage on them. However, the white man intervened and peace was restored. His investigation into the cause of the disturbance proved the Amaọkbam group guilty, and they were ordered to pay compensation to Nweke's people.

This atrocious conduct on the part of the Amakọbam group deprived many of Nweke's people of their means of livelihood. Those who could no longer continue with farm work took up other work under the white man, away from the town.

When a settlement had been reached in this farm dispute, some of the farmers returned to work on this land, but in future they spent more time on the farm, and arranged for a watch to be kept on their property whenever they were away.

But, meanwhile, the success of the first emigrants had encouraged many other people to 'go abroad', and soon the emigration threatened to depopulate the town.

MY FATHER GOES TO LAGOS

My father once told me the exciting story of his seven days' journey to Lagos.

His first sight of Lagos, he said, was a shocking disappointment. What he saw and experienced were contrary to his expectations. He had been told Lagos was a wonderful city, all the streets broad and paved with white gravel, and flanked with magnificent storeyed buildings. There were no thick bushes, but gardens with beautiful rosy flowers. The inhabitants were literate and held responsible posts in the white man's government. These workers were fashionable in dress and always wore their best suits. Nothing derogatory was heard about Lagos. But he found Lagos a land of beauty and slums; of riches and poverty; of literacy and illiteracy—good and bad alike. The fault, he said, was not in Lagos; it was in him—he was a victim of false education.

For the first phase of his journey, he trudged eighteen miles from his village to Onitsha. This was in the month of June, the peak of the rainy season. The day he set out for his four hundred-odd miles' journey started bright and beautiful. His luggage was a pair of shorts and a shirt. These he wrapped in a raffia bag, for he had no box. (In fact he had no need for one, as he had only a pair of shorts and a singlet for many months to come, and replaced them only when they were quite worn out.)

The District Clerk at Awka had told him to proceed to Onitsha and ferry across the river Niger to Asaba. There he would take a Government lorry to Lagos. He had gone about half-way to Onitsha when the weather changed. A fierce wind blew against him. The sky darkened. Thick clouds rolled overhead. There was thunder, followed by a heavy downpour of rain. He was not bothered, and kept up his walking speed. He was drenched. So also were the treasured contents of his parcel. Getting wet was, of course, no unusual experience for him, and the rain soon ceased. However, he was not happy carrying along a wet parcel. This problem was quickly solved. He picked up a long stick and laid it across his shoulder. At one end of the stick he hung his shirt; at the other, his pair of shorts. Sunshine came, and before he got to Onitsha both had dried. He made up his parcel again and felt happy.

The second phase of his journey was by canoe across the lordly River Niger—the first time he had travelled in any way except on foot. He carefully looked for what he considered the biggest canoe on the beach. It was a comfortable journey, and most of the time he was absorbed in admiration of the horizon and the wonderful works of nature around. On inquiry at Asaba, he found the lorry to take him to Lagos.

The Beginning of Mass Emigration

Early the following morning, he started the third and last phase of his journey—seven days' journey by lorry. This was in the early days of motor transport in the country. Only occasionally did lorries travel between Lagos and Asaba. The roads were bad. It was fair weather when they started, and for three days it was a pleasant journey. On the fourth day came a heavy rain, preceded by a strong wind and thunderstorm. The driver brought the lorry to a sudden stop and shouted that they were in danger. Within seconds, all the passengers had jumped out of the lorry. It had nearly crashed into a tree which had fallen across the road. The road was thus blocked. If they were to continue the journey, only two alternatives offered themselves—either another road would have to be built, or the tree cut up and the trunk moved. The latter was impracticable, and so the few passengers worked hard all day, in the humid weather, to build another road. (Drivers anticipated such obstacles and carried road-building implements.) In the night they were subjected to the cruel bites of mosquitoes. After two days of hard and relentless toil, they were able to build a by-pass, along which the journey was continued. They arrived in Lagos worn out.

HE LEARNS ABOUT LAGOS

Two days after his arrival, Nweke went out sight-seeing with a colleague of his. He had not seen much when his friend left him, to keep another engagement. My father would not give up, but chose to go on alone, trusting that he would find his way about by asking people.

At one time he felt lost, and decided to ask. If only he could get his bearings, he thought, he would be all right. Soon he saw a young man, well dressed in a striped cotton suit. He walked up to him and said, 'Excuse me, sir, would you please

H
113

direct me to the G.P.O.?' The young man gave him a cold, contemptuous look and replied 'Emi Ogbọ' (a Yoruba expression meaning, 'I don't understand') and went away.

My father looked perplexed. Although he did not understand what the young man had told him, he thought his gestures impolite. Next, he went to another person, older and better dressed. He listened and appeared to be nice, but he also said 'Emi Ogbọ', and other things which Nweke did not understand. This man did not walk away as the former had done, but stood gazing at him. My father, much embarrassed, stepped back and walked away. He was much disturbed. He hesitated to ask a third person. Walking up the street he pondered on his two experiences, feeling much disheartened. But presently relief came.

He was crossing a major road junction when a young man called out to him, 'Hello, Mr. Daniel!' and sped to meet him. The young man took him for a friend of his, a Mr. Daniel. When he discovered he was wrong, he apologized for the embarrassment caused him. They walked together and conversed. The young man introduced himself as Mr. Ige. 'No doubt you are a new arrival in Lagos?' asked Mr. Ige. 'Yes, I arrived only two days ago. I came out this morning with a friend, who has since gone back. I did not go with him, because I wanted to see more of Lagos.' 'And how do you like Lagos?' Mr. Ige asked. 'Well, Lagos is good but . . . by the way, are you a Lagos man?' Mr. Ige quickly replied, 'Yes.' 'Is "Mi Egbo" a Lagos expression?' my father asked. Mr. Ige at first looked puzzled. 'I see what you mean,' he said at length, 'but you haven't got the pronunciation right. It is "Emi Ogbọ", meaning "I don't understand".' 'Don't understand!' my father returned sharply. Mr. Ige continued, 'I would say you spoke to someone who replied in that way.' 'You are quite correct. It came not from just one, but two,

114

men.' There was a brief silence, and my father continued, 'I lost my way, and thought I should ask. I spoke to two well-dressed men, but, instead of the help I anticipated, I got a big rebuff. They did not speak English, but said "Emi Ogbọ", and other things I did not understand. Does this mean they did not understand the English language?' 'Maybe,' replied Mr. Ige. My father added, 'And one of them had a tie on!' 'Oh! I see you judged them by their appearance. Dress, I should tell you, my friend, does not mean anything here. People dress as well as they can afford. It is no mark of class distinction.' 'But I cannot think of any person in my area so well dressed, who does not speak good English,' my father remarked, shaking his head in wonder and disappointment. In the course of this conversation, my father learnt more about Lagos. He adapted himself to the circumstances of his new environment and soon the native vivacity of his face gave way to good-natured patience.

12. Marriage

The early emigrants first made their fortunes, and then, in conformity with tradition, made marriage their next concern.

After reaching the age of puberty, every man in Nweke's town was expected to marry sooner or later. It was believed that a man was not a fully responsible person until he was married. Marriage was not the concern of the prospective bridegroom only, but of his family as well. The family obtained an additional member, and this new member was expected to take part in all family matters.

BRIDE-PRICE

Marriage was contracted by means of 'bride-price', that is, a payment in money or in kind, made by the man to the father of the girl. The 'bride-price' was a test of the sincerity of the man who was asking for a wife. It was also a token on the part of the man that he was making the girl his partner and would take every care of her. These lines by the Reverend E. J. Hardy express the general opinion:

> *Use the woman tenderly, tenderly:*
> *From a crooked rib God made her slenderly.*
> *Straight and strong He did not make her*
> *So, if you try to bend, you'll break her.*

Bride-price assured the legality of the union of the man and woman and distinguished it from ordinary friendship. The acceptance of the bride-price by the father of the girl was a guarantee to the man that the girl became his wife, and that any children she bore would be his.

Bride-price in the days of Nweke's ancestors was purely in kind. The father of the girl required his daughter's fiancé, after his formal application, to cultivate his farm for a certain period. On completion of this service, he customarily declared the girl his wife. In time, this service changed to a payment in yams and livestock. This again changed to the payment of money, the sum involved being only a few bags of cowries in the late nineteenth century, but in 1964 the enormous sum of £200.

The present generation is not happy about the bride-price situation. I have no arguments in favour of high bride-price, for bride-price now acts as a deterrent to young men who wish to marry, since it is difficult for them to raise the sum of money required. Hence, many men cannot marry until well advanced in age. Others borrow money in order to get married, and are in debt from the beginning of their marriage, which leads to financial distress, misunderstanding between husband and wife, and unhappiness in their married life.

High bride-price also prevents men from taking the wife they prefer. For, by the time they have saved the bride-price, the girl may have already gone to a man whose money was ready sooner. High bride-price keeps many men and women bachelors and spinsters, and therefore encourages another social evil, prostitution. Today, every effort is being made to reduce the amount of bride-price.

MARRIAGE PROCEDURE

In contracting a marriage, a fixed customary procedure was

followed. When a young man met a girl he thought he liked, he would not proceed further until his parents or guardian had checked up on her antecedents. Were there any cases of insanity, leprosy, epilepsy, etc. in the girl's family? Were her parents and grandparents peaceable and co-operative? Information would be carefully sought on these points. The young man's relatives would also want to know what the girl herself was like, whether she was industrious and had a good physique and a cheerful countenance.

If they were satisfied about these matters, then the representatives of the family of the man made a formal approach to the father of the girl. The delegation was led by an intermediary, usually the person who had first recommended the girl. They took a pot of palm wine to the father or guardian of the girl as a token of betrothal, and explained the mission. The father of the girl accepted the palm wine, but did not give them a formal reply at that stage.

The father of the girl would then go through the same procedure of ascertaining the family history and personal merits of the young man. When he had done this, and consulted his relatives, and the girl, too, he sent to the intermediary to arrange a meeting between himself and his prospective son-in-law to determine the bride-price. In order to distinguish marriage from the market purchase of slaves, bride-price was never paid in full immediately; and, when the wife died, she was never buried in her husband's home, but taken back to her father's home and buried there. Payment of bride-price in instalments was normal, but as soon as the man paid the first instalment the girl formally became his wife.

The payment of the first instalment of bride-price was an important occasion. The prospective husband and his relatives took pots of palm wine to the father of the girl, who received them cordially and entertained them. When the man returned to his home, the girl accompanied him, carrying on her head one of the empty pots of palm wine brought by the man. She was sent to his home to see whether she would like to live there or not, and this also gave the relatives of the man a further opportunity to examine the qualities of the girl, and to decide whether she was suitable or not. After a native week, the girl returned to her parents to report how matters stood. If she was not satisfied, her father immediately returned the part of the bride-price already paid. If both parties were satisfied the contract was pursued, more bride-price was paid, some ceremonies were completed and the girl finally went to her husband's home.

Marriage contracted by this customary procedure could be summarily dissolved by either party by the repayment of the bride-price.

Nweke's Wife

Mgboye Enenmọ was the name of the girl who became Nweke's wife. She came from Urunnebo village in Enugwu-Ukwu town and was of noble parentage. She was born a few years after the coming of the white man. She took her name from the day of her birth, Oye. (Mgboye means daughter of Oye.) From childhood to womanhood her pleasant bearing and uncommon beauty, her good conduct and seriousness of purpose, her benevolence, wit and foresight earned her respect in the village.

After Nweke had completed the customary marriage procedure, he converted her to Christianity and sent her to school. The villagers were angry when their sons went to school, but they regarded it as an abomination for girls to go too, arguing that they would surely be corrupted. And so, when Mgboye started school, it caused a great sensation in the village. At school she learnt to read in the vernacular. After a time, Nweke sent her away from the village for further training in housewifery. Tutored by Mr. and Mrs. A. I. Williams, who came from Sierra Leone (as did most of the senior civil servants then), the village girl became a good baker, dressmaker and Europeanized housewife, and acquired some knowledge of the English and Efik languages.

Had a lesser woman married my father, he would not have prospered so well in both his private and public life. My father's weakness was his occasionally turbulent nature, and my mother always counteracted its devastating effect by her sense of inner calm. I see my mother as a woman who loved her husband and was determined to share his life. And to us, the children of this marriage, she gave the best of herself— that is, to myself, and to Chukwuebonamilo (female), Nwabueze (male), and Nebechianya (female). (That was the order in which we arrived.)

She had a large share in my father's happiness in his work; in his building a beautiful modern house in his village; and in his buying a house in the cosmopolitan town of Enugu. The acquisition of two such houses at that time was a remarkable achievement for a Civil Servant of his grade.

My mother believed that the home belongs to the woman, and she spared no effort to give us a home, a happy home that we are still exceedingly proud of.

How My Father Found My Mother

In 1923, Nweke wrote from Port Harcourt, where he was then working, to his elder brother at home, asking him to find a girl he could marry. When, in 1953, I had a long conversation with old Ezeuno of Enuagu, I put the question to him: 'If I were to write to you from Lagos, where I live, asking you to find a girl I could marry, how would you go about it to ensure you met my wishes?' A look of gloom passed over his face. He cheered up again, and said, 'My boy, I don't think that question can arise. You youngsters marry now without consulting your elders. Sometimes you fail to introduce your wife when you marry. Let's talk about something else, my boy. You should understand that things have changed.'

'I know things have changed, but that does not affect some basic customary procedures. They are still carried out in the village, aren't they?' 'I agree,' he replied, 'but I cannot see the possibility of your ever writing to us at home to ask us to look for a girl for you. Your present education and social status are beyond my comprehension. I can never find a girl suitable for you.' 'I am very sorry if I did not put my question properly. I simply want to know how you would go about such a task— just as you did in the case of my father. He wrote to his brother, didn't he?'

'I now understand what you mean and I feel happy.' He sat erect, beaming. 'You remind me of your father's marriage.' He fixed his eyes on me. 'What a pleasant reminiscence! Listen, my boy, your father's marriage was one of my greatest triumphs in life. When his elder brother got his letter, he told me about it. I was delighted. It gave me another opportunity to show my faith in that young man. Just then I had no girl in mind. For three days, I visited my most responsible friends, in-laws and relatives. At every place I visited, I carefully described the type of girl I wanted for your father. Where they had no one to recommend, they always promised to let me know if they thought of a girl. This initial effort of mine brought no material result, but I was satisfied in the knowledge that I had alerted my agents.

'Next, I visited important markets regularly, and kept a watchful eye open. I sought out and always attended dances

organized by teenage girls. It was time for the Afia Ebe, and I
went there. You must have heard of that. It was the public
marriage ceremony, just like your "wedding". The ceremony
has ceased with the increase of emigration and the influence
of the white man's ways. It was held at the Nkwọ market once
a year, towards the end of the dry season. All brides in each
village attended in their traditional bridal costumes. There
was music and dancing. After this ceremony they went to live
with their husbands. The brides of each village were accompanied by all the adolescent village girls, and young bachelors
had an opportunity to find a future bride for themselves.'

'What sort of girl were you looking for?' I asked. 'I was
looking for a girl from a good family; a girl of good height,
who possessed a calm, sweet, tranquil elegance. Such girls
have always proved good wives. Your father was a peaceable
man and I thought he deserved a partner with a similar
disposition.'

'How, then, did you succeed in finding the girl who was his
choice?' 'By chance I met a friend, who told me about her.
Her family was one I knew very well. A member of her
extended family was a good friend of mine. What I cannot
explain, my boy, is why this reputable family had previously
slipped my mind. It is still a mystery to me. Through the help
of my friend, I acquainted myself with the family and soon
became intimate with them. Then I saw a young girl, your
mother, at work in her parents' home. She satisfied all my
requirements. My friendship with the family grew. The
parents knew your father well, and were pleased when I told
them, informally of course, of my desire that he should marry
their daughter. The girl had known your father and gave her
consent to me in private. I informed your father's elder brother of my progress. The affair went forward. The girl occasionally visited me to collect palm wine for her parents. Our

village was famed for producing very sweet palm wine. I thought your father's elder brother had written to him of my success and I anxiously awaited his reply, so that we could make a formal approach to the parents. But something happened which caused me much embarrassment.

'One evening, your father's brother waded through heavy rain to my house. The broad smile on his face convinced me it was no bad news he brought. 'My brother has written,' he said, not waiting to sit down, "but we are going for a girl I have found, who is even better." "Better!" I ejaculated, terribly enraged, "What do you mean? Have a seat first." He sat down and I offered him palm wine. We drank and talked. He told me of the girl he had found. He insisted she was a better choice, and declared we ought to visit the parents formally. I quickly investigated, and came to the conclusion that the girl was not a suitable match for your father. Also, I found his brother stood to gain personally by the marriage. I thought he was not sufficiently disinterested. I told him I did not like his choice, and suggested we suspend the visit until your father arrived (he was due home on leave in about a month's time), so that he could decide for himself which girl was the better. However, the elder brother had the first say in the matter, and he exploited that privilege to have his own way. I did not go with them on the appointed day to visit the other family. I also refrained from causing any family dissension by openly challenging his judgment or making direct representation to your father. I already had a problem, and I thought I ought not to add to it. How could I now face my good friends, who had within the short period of my association with them discouraged two suitors, probably on account of my candidate? How could I make up to them for the embarrassment, I thought. It was a terrible feeling.

'The day after this visit, I summoned up courage and

confronted my girl's parents. I was stunned by their magnanimity. They advised me not to worry, and assured me the incident in no way affected our friendship.

'Nweke arrived. By special arrangement, his bride-to-be was presented to him. I was close to him, and noted his expression was unlike that characteristic of him when he was pleased. I felt sorry for him. Then I had the idea that he should see my own girl.

'At the earliest opportunity I told him all that happened and he indicated his wish to see my own girl. He put my representation before his brother, who urged him not to take any notice of me. But I knew I now had a chance to act, and felt absolutely confident of triumph. My girl was to come and collect some palm wine for her parents a few days after your father's return. This time, I did not leave the keg of palm wine in my house, but in your father's compound, and left a message for her to come and collect it there. She had never been to this compound before.

'In the evening, your father usually received and entertained his visitors in his family Obu (sitting house). I arranged my girl's visit for this time. Very briskly, my broadly smiling young girl walked into the compound. She was brilliant. She was gay. Beauty was hers. All eyes turned to her. I was pleased. I hurried to meet her, lifted the keg on to her head and sent her away. I had warned your father of the visit, and he saw her. He seemed frozen to the spot. His face, grim and haggard, was turned fixedly in one direction. The exuberance of the early evening was gone; he was deep in thought. I thought he would have a word with me, but he did not. When at last he retired to his room, I left for my house.

'At cock-crow the following morning, news reached me that he had had a quarrel with his brother in the night, and had finally told his brother to withdraw his own candidate.

Shortly after breakfast, he came up to me. At the front gate of my compound he called out to me. He wanted to know if it were not too late to resume talks for my girl. I told him that in the circumstances it might not be easy, as I knew her father was always firm on matters of principle. But if he so directed, I assured him, I would do my best even though it would mean really hard work. "Let's make a start at once," he said. "No delay! Employ every skill and all the tact at your command. You have my full support and I will reward you." He waited to see me get ready and go. "Shouldn't I go with you?" he asked as I was leaving. "No," I replied, "I will let you know when your presence will be useful."

'I opened negotiations, and my fears proved true. I first sought the co-operation of her mother. Her father was particularly fond of me and we often enjoyed long conversations together. That afternoon I was at my wit's end. I talked as amusingly as I could, and in fact dominated the occasion. I thought I had carried him away, and skilfully introduced the subject. But I did no more than arouse his dignity. Just one sentence from him left me puzzling and apparently defeated. "Young man, let's talk about other things, not that, please." I persisted. He insisted. I yielded.

'I made several attempts alone. Sometimes your father and I tried together, and sometimes your father alone, but never did the girl's father allow the subject to be introduced. All through your father's four weeks' stay at home, all efforts to discuss the matter with him proved abortive. He made it abundantly clear that his attitude on the subject did not in any way affect our friendship, but warned us that he must not be misunderstood. Your father went back to his post without a bride.

'Back at his post he inundated me and my girl's father with letters. I therefore persevered. In the end, by dint of constant attention and diplomatic conduct, I succeeded in reopening the matter with the father. That was how talks began concerning the girl who later became your mother.'

I thanked him for his brilliant account. Mainly to tease him, I asked another question. 'I have received the white man's education, just like my father. If you could find him a wife, I believe you could do the same for me.' He looked up and said laughingly, 'I think you are far more educated than your father. Even though your father had education, society at that time had not changed much, and hence the best girl in the village was good enough for him. But in your own case, not only have you been educated and learned the ways of Western civilization, but society has changed radically; as a result, I think the best village girl would not be suitable for you. What I can do for you is to tell you the names of our people who have grown-up daughters. You yourself will find out where they live, and which of the daughters is right for you. Then write to me, and I will organize the rest of the business. If, on the other hand, you find someone in any of the neighbouring towns, write to me just the same, and I will find out if all is well with the family before you proceed further.'

One point should be noted here. Nweke had no doubt seen many marriageable girls at Port Harcourt and elsewhere, but he was determined to marry a girl from his own town. This was in keeping with the tradition of his people, since it made it easier for each party to learn more about the family and personal reputation of the other. It was not considered honourable to marry a girl from abroad. However, this notion is now being challenged by the younger generation, who choose wives from farther afield, partly because of the unreasonably high bride-price at home.

Marriage

THE CHRISTIAN MARRIAGES

In 1925, at Port Harcourt, Nweke took Mgboye to the altar, and the nuptial knot was tied by the Reverend Okagbue. This form of marriage, by the Marriage Ordinance and with the blessing of the Church, was known as Church Marriage. As a result of Christian teaching, there was a growing desire among Christians for Church Marriage. This condemned polygamy, while customary marriage permitted it. A Church Marriage was an important ceremony, and a married person was not a full member of a Church until he had taken part in it. Women took particular care to have a Church Marriage, for it earned them the title 'Missis' (Mrs.), which raised their social prestige.

Though Nweke underwent a Church Marriage, he had completed the customary procedure before that. Indeed, it was not possible for a man to take a wife honourably in Nweke's town without going through the customary procedure. The Christian had therefore to satisfy two marriage systems—that requiring the customary marriage and that requiring the Church Marriage.

This state of affairs has been much criticized recently, since it means waste of time and labour, with much heavy expense, and makes no difference in the relationship between the man and wife. Opinions from various quarters go to show that many Christians are no longer in favour of this duplication of ceremonies. They feel that, since the two systems serve the same purpose, it should be enough to follow only the customary procedure, without adding to it.

13. The Christian Child

Most of Nweke's people who went abroad in the early 1920s were Christians, and their children were the first to be brought up under a largely Christian system of education. These children were sent to school when they were five, and later took jobs where their parents were living. Hence, some never visited their home village till they were grown up and had adopted Western ways of life.

The tragedy of it was that these carefully educated children, who had been given more attention than their counterparts in the home village, could not, when they returned, fit into the traditional social structure. They had been given personal names which had no connection with the system of names used in the village. Moreover, as they had lived most of their early life abroad, they had learnt to talk, not their mother tongue, but the white man's language, or the foreign language spoken where their parents lived. Even when they attempted to acquire their mother tongue, they were often unable to speak with the correct accent. It is very sad to meet a grown-up person who is fluent in the white man's language, but who can hardly say a word in his mother tongue without apologizing for mistakes.

At the beginning, parents did not understand what harm this ignorance would do in the cultural education of their children and in home affairs. But later they realized the mistake—when the appalling situation arose in which a young man did not fully understand his own language, was ignorant of his rights in the village, did not know his father's property, his own inheritance, and had no knowledge of the people and affairs of the village.

Strenuous efforts were made by parents and by the community to counteract these evils. Those who lived abroad sent their children back to the village to attend school, and to learn something about village matters. Young men who were working abroad regarded it as a duty to travel home whenever they had leave. And the town union made it binding on every citizen to return home with all the members of his family at a specified time.

THE CHRISTIAN CHILD BACK IN THE VILLAGE

Among the early Christian parents were my father and mother. I was the first son, and was born in the township of Port Harcourt, the seaport of the Eastern Region of Nigeria. My father gave me the long name Sigismund, meaning 'Conquering Protection'. It was his intention to express a particular circumstance by this name. If he had not been a Christian he could have done the same, more easily, with a native name. He found this name only after much research, and he thought it came closest to what he wished to express. None of his fellow tribesmen ever took this name, Sigismund, and many found it difficult to pronounce. They criticized him for overlooking the common Christian names and wondered where he found this one.

My father, shortly after my birth, worked in a non-Ibo speaking community where the lingua franca was the white man's language. As a result, I learnt to talk the white man's language. Till I was five years old, I could not say a word in my mother tongue.

I was five years old when I was taken by my father to Enugwu-Ukwu for the second time, the first time being when I was a little over a year old. The mere sight of the villagers and the strangeness of the environment alarmed me. My conduct was very amusing. When my paternal grandmother approached me to pick me up, I screamed wildly and ran away. I ran to my mother and cried, 'Mamma, look that dirty woman, who bi that? Ee dey touch me.' As I said this, I was shivering violently and would not look up. Poor me! it was the grandmother whom I later became very fond of, but I did not know her then. I next ran to my father and complained, 'Papa, which place bi this? Make we go now!' I was very uncomfortable during my stay in the village—although it was my own village! Poor me, I did not understand! I screamed whenever any villager came near me and did not allow most of them to touch me. No amount of persuasion from my parents could make me mix with the people. My conduct was the subject of much talk among the villagers. Their common remark was, 'Well, there is a Christian child, and that is how they behave!'

THE LONELY STRANGER

One incident during this visit is always fresh in my mind. It was my first experience of horror. For the first time, I saw adult men and women crying and wailing, and women throwing themselves on the ground. It happened one bright sunny morning. Somebody, I later learnt, had died in the adjoining village. He was a middle-aged man, one of the very few people I would talk to, who had also returned on leave, bringing with him his wife and two children. In the morning of the day previous to his death he was well, but in the afternoon he suddenly fell ill, and died the following morning. He had been very sociable and was loved by one and all. His sudden death was a great shock to all the villagers—hence the frantic expressions of grief, and the stampede to his house.

Within minutes, all the adults in our compound had rushed out to the compound of the deceased. I saw my grandmother running with her hands clutching her head. We children, the very little ones, were left behind.

The children, mostly about my own age, moved from one part of the compound to another, playing and enjoying themselves. There was no Papa, no Mamma, I could hang on to. I was scared to remain alone, so I trailed after the other children. They soon started leaving the compound. Where they were going, I did not know. At the front gate, I hesitated and I looked back. The compound was deserted. I had no alternative but to stay with them. I did not understand their language, and they did not understand mine. They made their way along a sandy path. Once, my foot sank into the sand. I thought I was falling into the ground, and was about to scream. Just in time, one of the children took me by the hand and pulled me out and along. Soon we left the sandy path, and started going through winding passages in the bush. The bright light was gone. It was a world of shades. I was horrified by the strangeness of this new world. I looked around, to see matted branches overhanging everywhere. I wanted to go back, but the view behind was equally terrifying. I was drawn on by the exuberance and cheerfulness of the other children. I was already ten yards behind, but two of them came back; one took my right hand, the other my left. I followed, my eyes half-shut in horror.

Next came a sharp turning to the left and I lost sight of the other children. They had raced down the adjoining slope, which led to the village stream. 'What sort of place is this?' I thought. I looked at the face of the boy on my right, then at the one on my left. They spoke to me but I did not understand them. They urged me on with encouraging gestures, and stepped down the first part of the very steep slope. Their step was firm—mine slipped. Then both feet slipped. Though they managed to hold me back, terror struck my heart. I was a victim of a dreadful misadventure, I thought. Papa and Mamma were not there to help me. Again I looked at the two boys, again I looked down the precipice.

At that unfortunate moment, I caught sight of the creature I most hated to see. It was a snake crossing the path. My declining courage was shattered. I screamed, and pulled my hands away from the two boys. I screamed at the top of my voice for Papa and Mamma to hear me and come to my rescue. The children down by the stream looked up, amused. When I looked for help and sympathy, they laughed at me. For quite a long time my screams mingled with the cries of the birds. I felt an intense hatred for anything connected with the adventure. I lost faith in the children because they laughed at me. When they could do nothing for me, they called their elders. The elders, as they approached me, started laughing too. 'They are just the same,' I thought. I had no confidence in them. All their efforts to pick me up failed. I was screaming all the time. But my saviour soon arrived. A real saviour, I thought; one of the only two who do not live with snakes in this horrible wilderness; who give me sympathy when I want it and do not show their teeth in laughter. It was my father. Peace had come to me again. He picked me up and asked, 'What ting dey do you?' 'This people, them take me for bush. I see snake. Bush people. Papa make we go.' Looking scornfully at those around, I crept into the circle of his protecting arms.

The Christian Child

I told my story to my mother. For the rest of the day I did not step out of our house. I refused to play with the other children, and whenever I saw those connected with my unhappy adventure, I would beckon to my mother, and say, 'Mamma, mamma, look them!'

After a brief stay, my parents left the village for a new station, Enugu, an Ibo-speaking town. I now had an opportunity to pick up my mother tongue. I mixed with my fellow children in play and at school, and gradually learnt to express myself in Ibo. Though circumstances did not permit my father to send me home to the village to attend school, and I continued to live abroad, I nevertheless visited home occasionally. I had little opportunity to associate closely with the villagers, but I made a special effort to become acquainted with local affairs, and later in life I championed the cause of the village in which, when I was five years old, I had refused to live.

14. Overthrow of the Warrant Chiefs

As we have seen, the government of the village was originally in the hands of the indigenous village council, the members of which lived in the village. With the advent of the white man, they were robbed of their authority by the Warrant Chiefs. Emigration began, and members of the village moved to townships and distant places for the purposes of trading and finding employment. These emigrants carried the tradition of the village meeting to their respective abodes abroad, where it continued to function as a social body. At home, too, the village council continued, though no longer as an executive authority, but only as a body concerned with purely social events. With the introduction of the Native Court and the overthrow of the indigenous leaders, the villagers no longer sent their cases and complaints to the village council but to the Native Court. Hence they soon lost that respect and fear of the elders which kept them well behaved and, as a result, numerous law suits were heard in the Native Court. For instance, husband and wife, instead of settling their disputes within the family in the traditional way, made an exhibition of themselves in the Native Court. These things were completely foreign to the village and soon shattered the basic spirit of goodwill and fellowship there. This, coupled with the corrupt conduct of those in authority, made the home atmosphere thoroughly unhappy.

Overthrow of the Warrant Chiefs

The members abroad were deeply troubled when they heard of these things. However, they could not individually, or through their small social meetings, control affairs at home. At Enugu, forty-seven miles away from Nweke's town, where the number of migrants from Enugwu-Ukwu had greatly increased, the people were bitterly dissatisfied with events at home and often wondered how they could improve the situation.

ENUGWU-UKWU PATRIOTIC UNION BORN

In 1942 Nweke, in consultation with some other members of his town, considered it worthwhile to call a general meeting and inaugurate an organization which would, firstly, deal with the welfare of its members in Enugu and secondly, as an enlightened and constitutional body, influence and intervene in affairs at home.

This was about the month of July, 1942. I remember this time not only as a turning point in the political and cultural advance of Enugwu-Ukwu, but also as a time when my knowledge of English increased.

My parents were living in their own house at Enugu, and I was with them for the mid-year holiday. For the first four days of my holiday, I observed that my father went out shortly after supper, and returned late. On the fifth day, I saw him go out again. I went straight to my mother and asked, 'Mamma, since I arrived, Papa has gone out every night and returned late. Please, where does he go to?' 'He goes to plan for a meeting they want to start.' 'What meeting is that?' And I added sarcastically, 'Is it the sort of meeting where people meet and drink? But Papa doesn't drink much!' 'No, it is not that,' she replied softly. 'It is a meeting for the welfare and good government of our town. They may start it very soon.'

It was Friday. My father did not go out that evening. He called me and told me about the meeting which was to take place on Sunday at 2 p.m., and charged me with the responsibility of getting ready a vacant room on the east side of the house for the meeting. He also sent me out to deliver circulars to six people. This task I carried out expeditiously and to his liking, and so won his wholehearted approval. Shortly after supper that evening, a young man came to see my father. He was one of his staff. He came to tell my father that he was not feeling well and would go to see the doctor the following morning. As a result he might be late or absent from work. My father looked sympathetic and commented, 'You look pale; what do you think it is?' 'The symptoms are those of pneumonia. I had it some time ago.' 'Then it's serious. Please take care of yourself, and I hope you will be well soon.' He took up a piece of paper and a pencil and made a note of his interview with the young man: 'Mr. A.B.C. reported ill. Pneumonia—to see Doctor tomorrow.' I was standing by him. He slipped the note into my hand and asked me to put it in the pocket of his working-shirt. The young man left. I took the note away, and read it; but instead of doing as I was told, I returned to my father with it. 'Papa,' I said, 'The young man told you he thought it was "neumonia" but here you have written a different thing, "pneumonia". That's a mistake, isn't it?' He took the note again and looked at it. 'No,' he said. 'It's no mistake. That is how pneumonia is spelt. The "p" is silent when you pronounce it.' He turned, gave me a searching look and continued, 'Does this mean you can't spell that word correctly? Have you ever seen it written down?' 'No,' I replied. 'But isn't it ridiculous that it should be pronounced so differently from the way it is written?' He smiled. 'Go and put the note away, and come back.' Soon I was back. He seized the opportunity to test my ability in spelling and the use of words. He made a list of some English words spelt differently from the way they are pronounced. 'You are not bad,' he said. 'I think you make no effort to look up words when you first hear them. Your pocket dictionary is not good enough.' My father taught me that night the basic approach to correct spelling and the proper use of the English Dictionary. Finally he promised to buy me a dictionary which he thought would serve me for that time and the future.

A Present From My Father

The next day, Saturday, my father rode back from work on his Raleigh bicycle, holding a book in his right hand. I met him and took his bicycle from him, as I usually did. I thought the book might be my new dictionary but I had not expected it so soon. In the house, he called me and handed the book to me. 'This is your dictionary,' he said. 'Use it well and you will grow and wax strong in knowledge.' 'Thank you, Papa,' I answered with a deep sense of gratitude. My joy knew no bounds. I hurried to my mother and showed it to her. 'That's very kind of him,' she said. 'Look after it, please.' It was a voluminous book—the first book of that size in my library. I had not opened it, but it had already endeared itself to me.

It was a busy afternoon for me. I was collecting chairs and forms, and I cleaned and washed some of them. After supper that evening, I put the finishing touches to my work. By bedtime, the room was ready for Sunday's meeting. I took my seat at one corner of the room and sat up till late at night looking through the book. I loved it at first sight. About midnight, my father observed that the light was on in the meeting room. I heard him comment, 'Sigis has gone to bed without putting out the light in this room.' Almost immediately, he opened the door. I saw his hand over the switch and the light went out. 'I have not slept, Papa,' I shouted. The light was put on again. He then peeped in and saw me, my new book right in front of me. 'I am very sorry then,' he said, and went away.

My father not only presented me with a book I valued very much; it was also associated in my mind with him. I wanted to possess a command of the English vocabulary, as my father did. I have always recollected the way he introduced the knowledge to me, and the profound force of spirit and dignity of thought he showed when he talked to his friends.

When I went back to school, I was the only pupil with so expensive a dictionary. I made good use of it and was respected. My pride was not negligible. The climax of excitement was reached when, one day, as I checked the spelling of a Christian name, I accidentally came across my own first name, Sigismund. I was immeasurably excited. I couldn't believe my eyes. I looked again—it *was* Sigismund. That was one of the most gratifying experiences of my boyhood days. My father had told me the meaning of Sigismund, which I considered a unique name, as I had never heard anybody called by it, or had even read of it. I was delighted when I found it, and knew its origin and history.

I felt a burning love for this book. I looked after it as I never did anything before. I revered it. I adored it. It was not until after the death of my father that I realized my feelings were aroused by the circumstances connected with the book. It was my father I loved. It was my father I revered. It was my father I adored.

The Inaugural Meeting

Sunday was the inaugural meeting day. At 2 p.m., almost all the seats were occupied by an enthusiastic crowd. The traditional breaking of kola nuts was soon over and my father

138

took the floor, his powerfully built and impressive person towering above his table, and he made a speech, a speech that still echoes in my mind. I have never ceased to recall his mellow, sweet voice and those expressive gestures of his, with their captivating effect.

'My fellow citizens,' he began, 'it gives me great pleasure to welcome you here this afternoon. When some of us went round to demonstrate the need for this meeting I hardly expected we would have such a full house. This response makes me believe that we really understand what is at stake. I hope that the more we discuss together our common problems, the more we shall understand them, and the more we shall be prepared to work hard to solve them.

'There was a time when no one from our town lived in Enugu. But gradually our numbers increased and today we are many. Here we are, for no other purpose than to find our daily bread. This does not imply that we did not live well in our old homes. In our villages we enjoyed a full life. And if the white man had not come, we could have continued with our happy village life. But we see that the world is subject to changes. The white man came with education and civilization, and our ideas and outlook changed. Even within the village we behaved in a different way. It was this change of outlook that gave us the courage to leave the village. We have no reason to blame ourselves for taking this course, for we know how much we have benefited financially and educationally.

'But I would like you to consider this question. Are our villages the same as they were before the white man came? Emphatically no! Even before we left the village we were aware of certain changes. Indeed, some of us were responsible for a number of these changes. But what we did was not harmful. Other changes—constant litigation, frequent quarrels, bribery and corruption—things completely foreign to our village—were the result of the machinations of a certain unpopular group of our people. Some of us, I am sure, were compelled to leave the village because of the power of these people. And now, here before us, are adverse reports from home about the conduct of these same usurpers of authority. I ask you this question: when will these things end? After due consideration, I can suggest an answer—when we have resolved to stop them!

'My fellow citizens, it is just a few decades since we came under the influence of Western Civilization. If, within this short period, chaos has invaded the village to such an extent, what can we expect in the future? If we sit with our hands folded and let matters get worse, what will be the verdict of our children, the leaders of tomorrow? They will find reconstruction even more difficult, because they know less than we do about the village past. This ignorance of our children is another thing we must correct. True, it is the fault of circumstances, but we cannot be completely exonerated if we do not attempt to keep them in touch with village affairs. Though I refrained in the past from taking part in village ceremonies, many of which are now dying out, I am beginning to feel that there was something valuable in certain of the ceremonies and that they should be revived and conserved.

'This union has two main objectives—to seek the interest of its members, and to seek the welfare of our town. When I look at your faces, I can see in them a sincere desire to begin the struggle for the restoration of happiness and tranquillity in our town. We might begin our operations by making certain that our representatives under the new system will be honest and wise persons.

'In conclusion, one thing has brought us to this meeting— love for our town, which is called patriotism. Anything we do because of this love will endure and flourish. Let us be sure, and let the coming generations know too, that it is on this foundation of love and co-operation that we are founding this union. The patriotic spirit has led many to sacrifice their lives for the good of their country, and their names now occupy a conspicuous place on the scroll of honour. I therefore feel it is right to associate the name of our union with this spirit of patriotism.

'Let us look back to the days of our illustrious ancestors, by dint of whose labour we enjoyed a happy village life. Today we are proud of them. What will the coming generations say of us? We can earn their approval if only we do something to make them say with pride, "This is my town, these are my customs; here I belong."

'My fellow citizens, with these few remarks I beg to move that this union be called Enugwu-Ukwu Patriotic Union.'

Greeted with vociferous cheers this proposal, among others, was accepted. Nweke was assigned the duty of drafting the first constitution of the union, which was adopted at a subsequent meeting. As the brain behind the organization, Nweke provided a commodious meeting-place for the union in his own house.

The inauguration of the Enugwu-Ukwu Patriotic Union was warmly welcomed by all the groups living abroad. The Enugu union, being the nearest to home and possessing a large membership, assumed the duties of a Headquarters and circulated information to other unions. It was the keenest desire of all the unions to restore order at home, but this was not possible until those then in authority had been removed.

THE UNION INTERVENES IN HOME AFFAIRS

Two years later an opportunity came. As a result of re-organization in the Native Court System, the District Officer at Awka notified Nweke's town that it should send five representatives to a new Appeal Court. On hearing of this, the Enugu union summoned a meeting at home and invited members who were living near home to take a hand in the selection of these five men. After the meeting in July 1944, the Secretary of the Enugu union sent a circular letter to all other unions, which said:

'It is the expressed wish of the General Meeting held at home on 5th July 1944 that this Circular Letter be sent to you and that you treat the same as urgent. . . .

'Gentlemen, it is a pity that the present bad situation of things at home has compelled us to think twice and take our present step. Enugwu-Ukwu today, having nursed such heavy numbers of her children to maturity should be recognized as one of the leading towns in Onitsha Province. But to her disappointment nearly all of her children live abroad and leave the management of her affairs in the hands of incompetent leaders under whom she groans for immediate relief.

'Shortly, the District Officer, Awka, has asked Enugwu-Ukwu to send in five members in the Appeal Court and two from other towns. He said he wanted intelligent people. Time is gone when our representatives in the Appeal Court should look for an interpreter. Time is gone when our representatives could not sign their names. Time is gone when our representatives could not say one thing and be responsible for it. We want no more of tyranny; we want no more of injustice for monetary gain; bribery must die and the oppression of the poor should live no longer.'

The Lagos union, like other unions which received this circular letter, expressed its satisfaction at the new move in a letter dated 31st July 1944:

'This union felt indeed indebted to your union for the wise and responsible outlook it is taking in what now affects our town. Such changes, as an end to the evil happenings at home, are coincidentally what this union in conjunction with all others, look up to as its final aim of existence. We cannot but feel happy that while we have been planning you had already started on the reconstruction.'

THE FIVE MEN ELECTED

At a meeting held at home on 13th August 1944, the five men were elected. To demonstrate the seriousness of the situation and to protect the new representatives, a series of by-laws were passed by the home meeting, as follows:

'1. Bribery prohibited: any one of these selected men found to receive bribe shall be reported to the District Officer and shall be punished with a fine of £5 5s. od. payable to the Union.

2. The selected members shall be in possession of Record Books into which they have to record the Court proceedings etc.

3. Any member found incapable, shall be recommended for removal from his seat and another able man put in his place.

4. Any selected member shall be truthful to both Government and his people. Failure to do this, he shall be recommended for removal from his official seat.

5. Any selected member shall avoid all manners of malicious acts.

6. Any person who plans evil against these five selected men, either directly or indirectly from home or abroad shall stand a fine of £5 5s. od.

7. Any selected member is to serve for two years when another election takes place provided his conduct is entirely satisfactory.'

OVERTHROW OF THE WARRANT CHIEFS

The District Officer was invited to a subsequent meeting held in the town on 7th July 1945, and an address of welcome was presented to him. The Secretary, reporting on the meeting in a circular letter dated 20th August 1945 said, *inter alia*:

'After reading an address of welcome to the District Officer we brought out Mr. X to him and stated that we the town owners wish this young man to represent Enugwu-Ukwu in the Native Court of Umunri and that we should like the corrupt Old Chiefs to be struck off from the court members so that our town will be in peace. The District Officer did agree with us at once and struck off their names from the Court Record Book.'

Eulogizing the union's success at home, he continued:

'There will be no fear again in the town of ours. Although those old so-called chiefs had tried their best to block our suggestion, God is with us and we overcame them. A very good foundation is now being laid by the E.P.U. The other neighbouring towns such as Nawfia, Abagana, Enugwu Agidi, Agukwu, Nimo are now trying to follow our example. The District Officer in charge of Awka Division and the Senior Resident of Onitsha Province had sent to us good lines of congratulations on the way we conducted our town affairs.'

THE OLD CHIEFS PLAN TO SABOTAGE THE UNION

A desperate attempt by the Old Chiefs to sabotage the efforts of the Union was now made. It is interesting to see how this was nipped in the bud. In a circular letter dated 18th September 1945, the Secretary of the Enugu Union reported the proceedings of another meeting held at home on 4th September 1945, and said among other things:

Overthrow of the Warrant Chiefs

'I have to inform you all that the said meeting came to a success. We had done many matters in the town to peaceful order for which the people in the town congratulated us. Two men created the greatest confusion. They are Y and Z. One of them Z was fined the sum of £5 5s. 0d. and on failing to pay was excommunicated from our Society. The details of his offence was sent to the District Officer and he made no objection and confirmed our action. The charges are bribery and false report against the E.P.U. before the Senior Resident, Onitsha Province at Udoka Abagana Appeal Court. He eagerly instigated that this meeting must stop and that the old methods of the Native Court must be revived. Upon this we expelled him and the whole town supported. Therefore as decided, any Enugwu-Ukwu born found with Z will be fined 10s. till further notice. The other man Y was fined £5 5s. 0d. and he paid it instantly. He bribed the town people to appoint him as Chief.'

ENUGU UNION CONGRATULATED

The members abroad were exceedingly joyful at the overthrow of the usurping chiefs. The Lagos union expressed its delight in a letter to the Enugu Union of 7th October 1945.

'This union expresses its indebtedness and records with enthusiasm the efforts of your union in our town. It looks as if this is the turning point of events and the beginning again of the age of peace and good neighbourliness of the town.'

When in September 1945 the news of the developments at home reached our soldiers at the war front in South East Asia—there, amidst the whirling and bursting shells and the hardships of war—the men from Enugwu-Ukwu found time to register their glad support. In a letter they wrote home, dated 20th October 1945, they said among other things:

'Accept our hearty thanks and congratulation for your marvellous achievements. Honestly you have laid down a very good example for the rest of our men at home and abroad. . . .

'Meanwhile, we hereby enclose the sum of £7 (seven pounds) cheerfully for the support of the meeting. We hope for more in the near future.'

All this illustrates the efforts of the people abroad (far and near) to bring peaceful government to the town once more. With the overthrow of the supporters of the old system, they achieved the first stage of reconstruction.

15. The Town Union at Work

Thus the Enugwu-Ukwu Patriotic Union came into being and regulated affairs in the town. Despite the fact that, like the system employing Warrant Chiefs, it was not a traditional organization, and its leaders were not necessarily the titled men or the traditional rulers, it succeeded. But the reason for its success was that, unlike the Warrant Chiefs, it had a mandate from the traditional rulers and enjoyed their confidence.

It can be seen from the previous chapter that all general meetings which took momentous decisions on town matters were held at home, where it was possible to consult with the village heads, whose opinions were always respected. As a result the village heads supported the union fully.

The union can now claim to represent traditional society. It has a dual function, to encourage modern community development projects in the town, and also to revive and conserve the best aspects of the village customs.

From 1942 to 1947 the union was decentralized, but the Enugu union undertook to inform unions abroad about events at home. In December 1947, at the General Conference, the constitution of the union was revised and provision was made for a centralized authority to co-ordinate the union activities at all stations. General Officers were elected, and Enugu was formally recognized as the Central Headquarters of the union.

Other centres were recognized as Group Headquarters for groups of unions. The Officers of the Group Headquarters are elected from the various unions which make up the group. The Grouping is as follows:

Aba Group (14 stations); Enugu Group (10 stations); Makurdi Group (11 stations); Zaria Group (14 stations); Ogoja Group (8 stations); Onitsha Group (11 stations); Otulu Group (3 stations); Lagos Group (6 stations).

It was agreed that in principle the Central Headquarters should be at home, but there was no objection to its being at Enugu, since the most competent members of the union live there. It is hoped that, when circumstances prove favourable, the Central Headquarters will be transferred home.

The unions are responsible to the Group Headquarters, which in turn are responsible to the Central Headquarters. This system facilitates prompt and effective administration. There are Group Meetings with representatives from member unions, and General Meetings with representatives from Group Headquarters.

COMMUNITY DEVELOPMENT PROJECTS

With this organizational pattern, the union commenced work in the town.

A market is the most important locality in a village. The union therefore gave its first attention to the replanning and proper maintenance of the Nkwọ market, the principal local market. An extension was made to the market and more suitable market stalls with stone pillars and zinc roofing were erected. The whole site now presents a pleasing picture. Men and women alike are delighted by the improvement.

The nearest Post Office to Nweke's town was four miles away and this caused much inconvenience. To overcome this handicap the union, in 1945, applied to the Postal Authority for a Postal Agency in the town. In 1948 this request was granted. The Postal Agency first functioned in a temporary building, but a year later the union put up a modern building to accommodate it. The Agency now provides full postal facilities.

The funds for these projects came mainly from the purse of the union, but the District Officer was able to help by supplying a quantity of building materials under the Government Development and Welfare Fund Scheme.

The union encouraged the construction of good roads in the village and assisted the schools with grants and loans.

LITIGATION IN THE COURT

While the union concerned itself with these projects, many members were at daggers drawn because of the constant litigation in the village. Any person was free to walk to the court to bring a case, and the union therefore blamed the Court for the state of affairs. It was the general opinion that, if cases were tried in the traditional way, the unhealthy atmosphere would disappear. It was therefore proposed that a rule be made to the effect that no member, abroad or at home, should lodge any non-criminal complaint against another member at the official court, but that instead he should appeal to the union, which represents the traditional organization.

While the proposal was being discussed the native court system was reorganized and the Umunri court in Nweke's town was removed to a neighbouring town, Abagana. This was in 1947. The union made the most of this opportunity. No sooner had the court ceased to function than the union purchased the court building from the Administration and converted it into a town hall. Since then the rule has been strongly enforced that no member of the town should litigate against another member in the court. Any complaints must go first to the branch union. If the complainant or the defendant is not satisfied with the decision of the branch union, he is at liberty to appeal to the Group Headquarters, where representatives from the group unions sit to hear the case and give a verdict. If still not satisfied, he may appeal to the Central Headquarters, where representatives from Group Headquarters give the final verdict.

These three stages of appeal ensure proper dispensation of justice. Any member who goes contrary to these proceedings is severely disciplined. The members today recollect with pride that within recent years most of their cases have been amicably settled in the traditional way whereas, before, they had to attend court and were at the mercy of court officials.

That was the first bold venture of the union to revive customary procedure, and it met with abundant success. It is generally agreed that better results are produced when cases are treated in this way than when they are tried in court.

These initial successes spurred the union to introduce more reforms to bring about a return to traditional practices.

THE GENERAL RETURN HOME

Many sons and daughters of the town lived abroad and returned home only occasionally. Some did not bother to return home. The union, apprehensive of the danger ahead if this situation were allowed to continue, enforced a rule that every citizen of the town, no matter how far away he lived, should return home at a scheduled time, to be known as the General Return Home. The principal aim was to afford an opportunity for a general reunion, which would promote better understanding in personal and public matters.

Records of all members abroad were kept, and it was ruled that failure to return would result in disciplinary action and a heavy fine. Traders and self-employed men (who make up the majority of those abroad) had to return with their wives and children. Employees who found it impossible to obtain leave were allowed to absent themselves on condition that they sent their dependants home.

The first General Return Home took place in December 1947. Public performances and meetings were organized, at which those who had not seen each other for many years were able to meet again. Momentous decisions were taken at mass meetings. The occasion was a great success.

The Second General Return was held in December 1950 and the Sixth in December 1962. It was at first decided that the Return should be held every two years, but for various reasons the period was later changed to every three years.

The union also proposes to organize scholarship and training schemes, but these have not yet been worked out in detail. Meanwhile, it controls elections for local government councils, advises the councillors, and disciplines them if they prove despotic.

The union also initiated the building of a cottage hospital. Work on this project commenced in 1959 and on the 20th December 1962 the hospital was opened by the Eastern Nigeria Minister of Health. To this end, the people contributed £20,000 and the Government made a grant of £15,000. Other proposals include the building of training institutions and the establishment of industries, either alone or in co-operation with other neighbouring towns, the main aims of these expensive schemes being to promote a healthy society, to make it possible for children to train in the locality longer than has been the case hitherto and to reduce emigration.

The white man, it should be noted, is completely kept out

of the picture. Instead, the new village organization is based on, and closely resembles, the original organization of the traditional, independent, republican village. The union which is in power makes use as much as possible of the traditional procedures and forms of administration.

16. Cultural Pride

The union made strenuous efforts both to revive the best traditions of the town and to encourage the improvements in community development suggested by western civilization. In the first task Nweke played a particularly prominent part.

CHANGE OF NAMES

As already stated, he had had considerable difficulty in finding a suitable foreign name for his first son. When his second child, a girl, was born, the same problem confronted him. This led him to reflect—does taking a native name in baptism prevent one from becoming a good Christian? He soon made up his mind to give his daughter a native name. He made his intention known to the priest, who saw no reason to object. And so at baptism he called her Chukwu-ebonamilo which means 'let God not mark me out'. The church members were unhappy about this change and felt Nweke had done wrong. But it was not long before others understood his idea and followed suit. Some churches make it compulsory for their members to take a foreign Christian name in baptism, but then the parents call the child, not by the foreign name, but by his second native name. Many adults who were called by a foreign name have recently, through a legal process, changed such names for native names, the meaning of which they understand. In the issue of the *West African Pilot* of the 2nd April 1949, a member of Nweke's town advertised as follows:

Change of Name
I, formerly known as Felix Osita Nworjih, now wish to be known and addressed as Nwude Osita Nworjih from the 2nd of April, 1949. All documents bearing my former name remain valid.

N. O. Nworjih

RECOGNITION OF CUSTOMARY PROCEDURE

There appears now to be general agreement that there is nothing bad in many customary procedures, and many Christians once again take pride in carrying them out.

Title-taking is no longer the exclusive concern of the non-Christians. Many Christians prominent in various walks of life abroad have returned home to take a title. In fact, they have found it absolutely necessary, as their attainments abroad do not alone earn them recognition at home. Title-taking was never an evil custom, but rather the opposite, for a title was a symbol of sincerity and nobility. But Christianity as practised in this area interpreted it wrongly.

Christians and non-Christians alike now express equal enthusiasm for ceremonial feasts and indigenous sports contests. Native attire is no longer despised by the Christian class. The ideal of the customary marriage is now valued and the system again popular. The elders are no longer looked down on with contempt because they are non-Christians, but are restored to their former position of regard as the representatives of the ancestors, the fountain of goodness.

That a people which once succumbed to western civilization, and abandoned its own traditions, should now cautiously retrace its steps is testimony to their high degree of self-regard and common interest. They respect both themselves and their ancestors: they respect the blood tie which is the basis of their community and of their culture.

Nweke's Last Days

Wherever they lived abroad, Nweke's people showed their patriotic spirit by helping one another when difficulties arose and by always striving for the welfare of their town.

Nweke's last days were an opportunity for the people to demonstrate love and respect for their comrade, for one who was a principal pioneer in the progressive development of the town.

In 1943 Nweke became seriously ill while at Kano. How he survived was a mystery, for at one moment it appeared that his breathing had stopped, and an official telegram was despatched from his department to his next-of-kin announcing his death. But the hospital staff, his wife, his fellow townsmen and friends nursed him untiringly, for which they deserved the highest commendation.

When he recovered, in February 1944, he was granted leave and transferred to the south. In March he reached home again. The news of his return stirred the whole town, for it had been rumoured that he was dead. Speaking to his kinsfolk, who were exceedingly joyful over his return, he said among other things, 'Give glory to God. Thank my wife. My people at Kano are great patriots. My friends are true.'

He completely recovered and recommenced his evangelization, spreading the gospel of co-operation and love. He visited many neighbouring villages and towns. All were astonished to see him more robust and fresh than ever before.

But about the time he was due to resume duty at Enugu, he fell ill again. He was removed to the General Hospital at Onitsha, but his hour had come and no human power could change it. And so, in the early hours of the 5th May 1944 it was his turn to rest in peace. He died leaving 'footprints on the sands of time'. The following day he was buried with his ancestors at his home. His wife, his four children, all the people of his town and his many friends mourned for him.

GOD-FEARING, UPRIGHT AND HUMBLE

This was the end of the man who had held up the torch of progress in his town. From childhood he had shown great determination and courage. In his youth, he fought to go to school. In manhood he led the battle for the emancipation of his town from the yoke of despotic rule.

Ezeuno, who knew him when he was young, found him endowed with wit and foresight, soberness of speech and cheerfulness of disposition. He grew up God-fearing, upright, and humble. He was a great nationalist and statesman, and at the same time a sound and keen business man.

He lived a planned life, and, dying, he left directions for his family's future life. 'Do not send a telegram to Sigis. Write to the Principal and do not allow him to interrupt his studies and come home,' was his last whisper to my mother. 'I have told you the whole position. Be courageous and take care of yourself and the children.' Earlier, he passionately drew my mother closer to him. 'I want to talk to you,' he said, 'only assure me you will not start crying.' My mother gave the assurance trembling and afraid.

That was in my second year at the Abeokuta Grammar School. My father had used his intuitive power to avert any family crisis immediately after his death. Just before he fell ill the second time, he wrote to me and said he had paid my tuition and boarding fees for the whole of 1944. He added words of advice and encouragement; it was a very fine letter indeed—I think the best he ever wrote to me—and I was very pleased. But I wondered why he should pay a whole year's fee. I saw no justification for this and interrogated him. 'Why, Papa, why?' I wrote, anxiously hoping for a reply. I did not realize he had bade me adieu, and that I was writing my last letter to him.

My father was a strong Christian and a builder of the church in his town. He was a great lover of education and any brilliant scholar was sure of his favour. He was much grieved to see children who were not sent to school. Despite his limited resources, he was able to help many of his relatives and friends to acquire education. He was friendly to everyone, but had a few specially intimate friends.

On his sick bed, he discussed the affairs of the union with another staunch member. He expressed his absolute confidence in the capacity of his people, but added that if progress was to continue, the leaders must plan well and must give selfless service with unfailing sincerity, so that the people might continue to have confidence in them.

While he recognized the progress brought about by western civilization he repudiated the tendency of his people to forsake tradition completely.

And, of course, he was right. As individuals differ in character, so do states in their cultural outlook. One cannot, for any reason, completely abandon one's culture to make room for another. There must be a spirit of give-and-take in cultural matters. Peoples and nations, like individuals, pride themselves on their peculiar characteristics.

The white man came to our people with a way of life quite different from our own. At first, to achieve his objective quickly, he pressed his own way of doing things upon us. But when we abandoned our traditions in order to adopt his, the result was chaos. The white man learnt a lesson from this and modified his methods, but the influence of his ways had completely disrupted our social order. The harm was done. No lamentation could provide an immediate remedy. Yet something had to be done to put matters right. Whose responsibility was this? The white man's or ours? Unquestionably ours. Nweke, answering a similar question in his inaugural speech, proclaimed that we could put an end to the evil—'when we have resolved to stop it'. Nweke's generation slowly began to realize where they stood, and inaugurated a revival of tradition. Now we must ask what can be done by the present generation, the young men and women living today?

Not enough attention is being given to this matter at present. Our thoughts are absorbed in unrealistic discussions about capitalism, communism and other such topics. We study the history of other nations and we are taught to admire the courage and adventurous spirit of their heroes. At the same time, we forget that we too have historical origins; we too have heroes equally courageous, heroes full of an equally adventurous spirit. We too have men of noble mind whose life histories and philosophies of life could serve as a great inspiration to our youth. It is, however, gratifying that some of our primary school syllabuses are now being revised with some emphasis on local history.

It is, of course, very necessary for us to know what other people do; but how can we make the best use of the experience of others if we do not sufficiently understand ourselves? Self-knowledge is the beginning of wisdom.

And since our grandsires live in us, to know ourselves we must know them!

We want a Nigerian culture in an independent Nigeria.

Cultural Pride

What then do we understand by a Nigerian culture? Is it the culture of our cosmopolitan township? No! These communities are unrepresentative. Where then do we find our culture? We find it in our villages—there is the reservoir of our cultural heritage.

To the youth of these villages, therefore, this book is dedicated.

The hour is theirs, to rescue and to revive those good traditions which have been lost. Perhaps it is the last chance. For in any Ibo village today, there remain only a few who can remember distinctly the 'old world' and who can supply accurate information about our remote past. These old men will gladly tell us what we wish to know—but only if the present generation puts the questions.

In a few years, these survivors will be no more. Should their knowledge of things past not be handed over to the present generation, our history will be lost. Since no records were kept, it is only from the old men that we can learn about our past.

It is not always easy to follow the stories told by the old men. They relate haphazardly events associated with different ancestors. And it is not safe to rely on the unsupported memory of only one man; it is essential to put the same question to as many men as possible, and then to weigh the answers. The task takes time, and is sometimes tedious. But it is well worth while.

For our knowledge of the past will illuminate our present path to a greater future.

Our culture is our heritage and our pride.